Marriage and Partnership

Series Editor: Cara Acred

Volume 244

Independence Educational Publishers

First published by Independence Educational Publishers

The Studio, High Green

Great Shelford

Cambridge CB22 5EG

England

© Independence 2013

Copyright

Photocopy licence

British Library Cataloguing in Publication Data

Marriage and partnership. -- (Issues ; 244)

1. Marriage. 2. Family. 3. Unmarried couples.

I. Series II. Acred, Cara editor of compilation.

306.8'1-dc23

ISBN-13: 978 1 86168 646 6

Printed in Great Britain

MWL Print Group Ltd

Contents

Introduction

Marriage and Partnership is Volume 244 in the *ISSUES* series. The aim of the series is to offer current, diverse information about important issues in our world, from a UK perspective.

ABOUT MARRIAGE AND PARTNERSHIP

Many people view marriage as an age-old institution, steeped in tradition. In today's society, however, opinions on marriage and partnership are being challenged and ideas are rapidly evolving. Critics of same-sex marriage suggest that redefining marriage would undermine its ideals, but what does 'marriage' really mean? This book examines contemporary issues surrounding the marriage debate; presenting a variety of opinions, facts and statistics. *Marriage and Partnership* also considers the process of divorce, or ending a civil partnership, and raises important topics such as forced marriage and child marriage.

OUR SOURCES

Titles in the *ISSUES* series are designed to function as educational resource books, providing a balanced overview of a specific subject.

The information in our books is comprised of facts, articles and opinions from many different sources, including:

* Newspaper reports and opinion pieces

* Website factsheets

* Magazine and journal articles

* Statistics and surveys

* Government reports

* Literature from special interest groups

A NOTE ON CRITICAL EVALUATION

Because the information reprinted here is from a number of different sources, readers should bear in mind the origin of the text and whether the source is likely to have a particular bias when presenting information (or when conducting their research). It is hoped that, as you read about the many aspects of the issues explored in this book, you will critically evaluate the information presented.

It is important that you decide whether you are being presented with facts or opinions. Does the writer give a biased or unbiased report? If an opinion is being expressed, do you agree with the writer? Is there potential bias to the 'facts' or statistics behind an article?

ASSIGNMENTS

In the back of this book, you will find a selection of assignments designed to help you engage with the articles you have been reading and to explore your own opinions. Some tasks will take longer than others and there is a mixture of design, writing and research-based activities that you can complete alone or in a group.

FURTHER RESEARCH

At the end of each article we have listed its source and a website that you can visit if you would like to conduct your own research. Please remember to critically evaluate any sources that you consult and consider whether the information you are viewing is accurate and unbiased.

Chapter 1

Marriage & cohabitation

Getting married

Who can get married

According to the law of the United Kingdom, a man and a woman may marry if they are both 16 years or over and free to marry, that is, if they are single, widowed or divorced, or if they were in a civil partnership which has been dissolved.

In the United Kingdom people cannot marry if they are:

⇨ aged 16 or 17 who do not have parental consent

⇨ people of the same sex. However, a same-sex couple can register a civil partnership instead, which will give the partners many, if not all, the rights of married couples. For transsexual people, the relevant gender is the one on their current birth certificate

⇨ certain relatives.

Young people

If you are 16 or 17 you cannot marry without parental consent. Each parent with parental responsibility is entitled to give parental consent. In some circumstances, other people may give parental consent. In Northern Ireland a young person under 18 cannot marry without the consent of certain people.

For more information about who can give parental consent, you should consult an experienced adviser; for example, at a Citizens Advice Bureau. To search for details of your nearest CAB, including those that can give advice by email, go to our website and click on 'nearest CAB'.

Transsexual people

A transsexual person who has applied for and has been granted a full gender recognition certificate by the Gender Recognition Panel can get a new birth certificate which reflects their acquired gender. They will then be able to marry someone of the opposite gender to their acquired gender. However, if a transsexual person does not have a gender recognition certificate, they are legally considered to be the gender that is on their original birth certificate. They will not be able to marry someone of the opposite gender to their acquired gender.

Where can a marriage take place

A marriage can take place in:

⇨ a Register Office

⇨ a church of the Church of England, Church in Wales, Church of Ireland, Presbyterian or Roman Catholic Church in Northern Ireland

⇨ a synagogue or any other private place if both partners are Jewish

⇨ a Meeting House if one or both partners are either members of the Society of Friends or are associated with the Society by attending meetings

⇨ any other religious building provided that the person marrying the couple is registered by the Registrar General – see under Religious marriage ceremonies (England and Wales only)

⇨ premises approved by the local authority – see under Religious marriage ceremonies (England and Wales only)

⇨ a place where one partner is seriously ill and not expected to recover

⇨ the home of one of the partners if the partner is housebound; for example, has serious disabilities or is agoraphobic

⇨ a hospital, if one of the partners is unable to leave or is detained there as a psychiatric inpatient

⇨ a prison, if one partner is a prisoner.

Local authority approved premises (England and Wales only)

Local authorities in England and Wales may approve premises other than Register Offices where civil marriages may take place. Applications for approval must be made by the owner or trustee of the building, not the couple.

The premises must be regularly open to members of the public, so private homes are unlikely to be approved, since they are not normally open to the public. Stately homes, hotels and civic buildings are likely to be thought suitable. Approval will not be given for open air venues, such as moonlit beaches or golf courses. Generally, the premises will need to be permanent built structures, although it may be possible for approval to be given to a permanently moored, publicly open boat. Hot air balloons or aeroplanes will not be approved.

If you want to get married in local authority approved premises you should obtain a list of premises from the local town hall. Or you can search for approved premises on the General Register Office's website at: www.gro.gov.uk.

How to marry

You can get married by a civil ceremony or a religious ceremony.

In both cases, the following legal requirements must be met:

⇨ the marriage must be conducted by a person or in the presence of a person authorised to register marriages in the district

⇨ the marriage must be entered in the marriage register and signed by both parties, two witnesses, the person who conducted the ceremony and, if that person is not authorised to register marriages, the person who is registering the marriage.

Civil marriage ceremonies

You and your partner must give notice of marriage in your local Register Office, whether or not you wish to marry in that district. The Superintendent Registrar or Registrar in Northern Ireland then issues authority for the marriage and you may marry in any Register Office or local authority approved premises in any district.

If either you or your partner is from overseas, special rules may apply when giving notice to marry. If so, you should consult an experienced adviser, for example, at a Citizens Advice Bureau.

In the period between the notice of intention to marry and the ceremony, anyone with strong grounds for objecting to the marriage can do so. Making a false statement is a criminal offence.

In England and Wales, both partners must be resident in England or Wales for seven days before notice is given (on the eighth day). A notice must state where the marriage is to take place. The marriage can then take place after 15 days have elapsed from the date on which notice of the marriage is entered in the marriage notice book. There is a fee for giving notice. There is no requirement for the 15-day notice period if one of the partners has been issued with a gender recognition certificate and was previously the civil partner of the person who they wish to marry. In this case, notice of the marriage and the marriage itself can happen on the same day.

In Northern Ireland, a marriage licence is called a marriage schedule. Couples do not need to have been resident in the country before getting married, provided they apply for notice from the General Register Office.

If you and your partner are visiting Northern Ireland to be married and are citizens of a country that is not a member of the European Economic Area, you may need to enclose special documentation.

Couples must submit their completed marriage notice forms and any other relevant documents to the Registrar of Marriages in the district where the marriage is to take place.

It is normal to give eight weeks notice. However, you can give a minimum of 14 days notice, although this may mean that the wedding ceremony will have to be postponed. The registrar will issue a marriage schedule. You won't be able to get married without this. If you are having a religious ceremony, this must take place within 14 days of receiving the schedule. In addition to this, the schedule must be signed at the religious ceremony by the person performing the marriage.

The marriage must take place within 12 months from the date of entry of the notice (three months if one of you is housebound, detained or resident in Scotland or Northern Ireland). If the marriage does not take place within that time, the process must be repeated.

Religious marriage ceremonies (England and Wales only)

The Church of England and the Church in Wales are allowed to register a marriage at the same time as performing the religious ceremony.

Ministers and priests of all other religions can be authorised to register marriages and must have a certificate or licence to do so from the local Superintendent Registrar. For Jewish and Quaker marriages, the authorisation is automatic. For all other religions, if the official performing the ceremony is not authorised, either a Registrar must attend the religious ceremony or the partners will need to have separate religious and civic ceremonies.

Religious ceremonies and civil ceremonies

If a couple has been married in a Register Office in England, Wales or Northern Ireland, the partners can have a religious marriage ceremony afterwards. The partners are likely to be asked for their marriage certificate. A religious ceremony which does not comply with the conditions stated above and which takes place before a civil wedding is not a valid marriage under United Kingdom law and the couple's status will be that of cohabitees.

Polygamous marriages

A polygamous marriage is one where a man can marry more than one wife. A polygamous marriage between partners, one or both of whom are domiciled in England, Wales or Northern Ireland is not valid. The concept of 'domicile' is very complex and does not necessarily mean 'living in' a country.

If you need to know about the validity of a polygamous marriage, you should seek specialist legal advice.

Marriages which are not valid

Certain marriages are treated as if they never took place. These are called void marriages. They are marriages which do not meet the requirements of United Kingdom law. An example of a void marriage is one where the partners may not marry because they are related.

Some marriages may have met the requirements of United Kingdom law when they took place but may then be annulled. These are called voidable marriages. There are a number of situations where marriages are considered voidable, for example if one partner has been granted a full gender recognition certificate (see under Transsexual people), or if one of the partners did not give valid consent to the marriage because the consent was given under duress. Either partner can seek to annul the marriage but if neither partner does, the marriage will be valid.

Bigamy

If you marry in the United Kingdom and are already legally married, the marriage will be bigamous and therefore is void. Although it is a criminal offence to marry someone when you are already married, prosecution is not automatic.

Remarriage/second marriage

As long as the legal requirements are met, there is nothing to prevent you from marrying again in a civil ceremony in the UK if you are widowed or divorced or if you were in a civil partnership that has been dissolved.

Religions have different rules about whether someone can remarry in a

religious ceremony. If you or your partner has been married before, or has been in a civil partnership that is now dissolved, and you want a religious ceremony, you will need to check with an official of the relevant religion.

Blessing ceremonies

Even if you are not allowed to marry in a religious ceremony, for example, because you belong to a religion that does not permit marriage of people who are divorced, it may be possible to arrange for your relationship to be blessed in a religious ceremony. This is at the discretion of the religious official concerned.

Forced marriages

A forced marriage is where you are pressurised into it against your will. You may be emotionally blackmailed or physically threatened, usually by your family. It is not the same as an arranged marriage, where both parties agree to the marriage.

Forced marriage is a criminal offence. If you are afraid that you may be forced into a marriage, you should contact the police or the Forced Marriage Unit.

You can also contact the Honour Network Helpline which advises victims of forced marriages and honour crimes. The helpline number is: 0800 5999 247.

If you are being forced into marriage or are already in a forced marriage, you can also get legal protection by

applying to the county court for a Forced Marriage Protection Order.

This order forbids families from:

⇨ taking you abroad for marriage

⇨ taking your passports away

⇨ intimidating or using violence against you.

It can also require family members to reveal where you are. The police can also apply for a Forced Marriage Protection Order. If someone breaks the order, they could be sent to prison for up to two years.

You should get legal advice as soon as you can. You may get legal aid.

Also, if you are afraid that you or someone else may be forced into marriage overseas, you should, before travelling, contact the address below for advice.

Forced Marriage Unit

Foreign and Commonwealth Office

King Charles Street

London SW1A 2AH

Tel: 020 7008 0151

Email: fmu@fco.gov.uk

Website: www.fco.gov.uk

⇨ The above information is reproduced by kind permission of Citizens Advice 2013. Please visit www.adviceguide.org.uk for further information.

© Citizens Advice 2013

How marriage has changed over centuries

Critics of gay marriage see it as an affront to sacred, time-tested traditions. How has marriage been defined in the past?

Has marriage always had the same definition?

Actually, the institution has been in a process of constant evolution. Pair-bonding began in the Stone Age as a way of organising and controlling sexual conduct and providing a stable structure for child-rearing and the tasks of daily life. But that basic concept has taken many forms across different cultures and eras. 'Whenever people talk about traditional marriage or traditional families, historians throw up their hands,' said Steven Mintz, a history professor at Columbia University. 'We say, "When and where?"' The ancient Hebrews, for instance, engaged in polygamy – according to the Bible, King Solomon had 700 wives and 300 concubines – and men have taken multiple wives in cultures throughout the world, including China, Africa, and among American Mormons in the 19th century. Polygamy is still common across much of the Muslim world. The idea of marriage as a sexually exclusive, romantic union between one man and one woman is a relatively recent development. Until two centuries ago, said Harvard historian Nancy Cott, 'monogamous households were a tiny, tiny portion' of the world population, found in 'just Western Europe and little settlements in North America'.

When did people start marrying?

The first recorded evidence of marriage contracts and ceremonies dates to 4,000 years ago, in Mesopotamia. In the ancient world, marriage served primarily as a means of preserving power, with kings and other members of the ruling class marrying off daughters to forge alliances, acquire land, and produce legitimate heirs. Even in the lower classes, women had little say over whom they married. The purpose of marriage was the production of heirs, as implied by the Latin word matrimonium, which is derived from mater (mother).

When did the church get involved?

In ancient Rome, marriage was a civil affair governed by imperial law. But when the empire collapsed, in the 5th century, church courts took over and elevated marriage to a holy union. As the church's power grew through the Middle Ages, so did its influence over marriage. In 1215, marriage was declared one of the church's seven sacraments, alongside rites like baptism and penance. But it was only in the 16th century that the church decreed that weddings be performed in public, by a priest, and before witnesses.

What role did love play?

For most of human history, almost none at all. Marriage was considered too serious a matter to be based on such a fragile emotion. 'If love could grow out of it, that was wonderful,' said Stephanie Coontz, author of *Marriage, a History*. 'But that was gravy.' In fact, love and marriage were once widely regarded as incompatible with one another. A Roman politician was expelled from the Senate in the 2nd century B.C. for kissing his wife in public – behaviour the essayist Plutarch condemned as 'disgraceful'. In the 12th and 13th centuries, the European aristocracy viewed extramarital affairs as the highest form of romance, untainted by the gritty realities of daily life. And as late as the 18th century, the French philosopher Montesquieu wrote that any man who was in love with his wife was probably too dull to be loved by another woman.

When did romance enter the picture?

In the 17th and 18th centuries, when Enlightenment thinkers pioneered the idea that life was about the pursuit of happiness. They advocated marrying for love rather than wealth or status. This trend was augmented by the Industrial Revolution and the growth of the middle class in the 19th century, which enabled young men to select a spouse and pay for a wedding, regardless of parental approval. As people took more control of their love lives, they began to demand the right to end unhappy unions. Divorce became much more commonplace.

Did marriage change in the 20th century?

Dramatically. For thousands of years, law and custom enforced the subordination of wives to husbands. But as the women's-rights movement gained strength in the late 19th and 20th centuries, wives slowly began to insist on being regarded as their husbands' equals, rather than their property. 'By 1970,' said Marilyn Yalom, author of *A History of the Wife*, 'marriage law had become gender-neutral in Western democracy.' At the same time, the rise of effective contraception fundamentally transformed marriage: Couples could choose how many children to have, and even to have no children at all. If they were unhappy with each other, they could divorce – and nearly half of all couples did. Marriage had become primarily a personal contract between two equals seeking love, stability and happiness. This new definition opened the door to gays and lesbians claiming a right to be married, too. 'We now fit under the Western philosophy of marriage,' said E. J. Graff, a lesbian and the author of *What Is Marriage For?* In one very real sense, Coontz says, opponents of gay marriage are correct when they say traditional marriage has been undermined. 'But, for better and for worse, traditional marriage has already been destroyed,' she says, 'and the process began long before anyone even dreamed of legalising same-sex marriage.'

Gay 'marriage' in medieval Europe

Same-sex unions aren't a recent invention. Until the 13th century, male-bonding ceremonies were common in churches across the Mediterranean. Apart from the couples' gender, these events were almost indistinguishable from other marriages of the era. Twelfth-century liturgies for same-sex unions – also known as 'spiritual brotherhoods' – included the recital of marriage prayers, the joining of hands at the altar, and a ceremonial kiss. Some historians believe these unions were merely a way to seal alliances and business deals. But Eric Berkowitz, author of *Sex and Punishment*, says it is 'difficult to believe that these rituals did not contemplate erotic contact. In fact, it was the sex between the men involved that later caused same-sex unions to be banned.' That happened in 1306, when the Byzantine Emperor Andronicus II declared such ceremonies, along with sorcery and incest, to be unchristian.

1 June 2012

⇨ The above information is reprinted with kind permission from *The Week*. Please visit www.theweek.com for further information.

© *The Week Publications, Inc. 2013*

Marriage and partnership: legislative landmarks

1970

People who have undergone gender reassignment surgery are not allowed to marry.

1982

'Forced' marriages are declared to be against the law where either the husband or wife has been forced to get married against their will, and has been placed under significant physical or emotional pressure to do so.

2002

The ban on marriages of transsexuals is challenged unsuccessfully at the European Court of Human Rights.

2004

English law changes to allow those who have undergone gender reassignment surgery to have their new identities recognised by law. This means they can now lawfully get married.

2004

The law changes to allow same-sex couples to register their relationships with the State from December 2005. This means that they will receive almost exactly the same rights and responsibilities as heterosexual couples when they get married.

2005

The Home Office declares that forced marriages are a form of domestic violence and an abuse of human rights.

2006

The Law Commission puts pressure on the Government to change the law so as to protect the financial interests of those who live together without getting married or registering their civil partnerships. The Commission proposes an 'opt-out' scheme whereby those who share a home or have a child together and make a contribution to the relationship which has long-lasting consequences when the relationship breaks down will be entitled to share property. Couples can opt-out by agreeing in writing to do so.

2012

The Government launches its consultation on equal marriage in England and Wales.

2013

The Same Sex Marriage Bill is first read in the House of Commons.

What do women want? To be married, of course

Statistics and surveys may show that getting hitched is falling out of fashion but, as soon as children come along, every woman would rather be wed.

By Judith Woods

Are you sitting comfortably? Or at least sitting? Because further down this page I am going to make the sort of bold, incendiary statement that will divide – but also, I hope, unite – couples at a moment when a blizzard of anti-marriage headlines makes it almost impossible to discern a future for an institution that has been a cornerstone of our society.

First, a little background. According to research from the Centre for Social Justice, marriage is being abandoned to the point where it's estimated that by 2031 only 57 per cent of families will be headed by a married couple, falling to just 49.5 per cent by 2047.

But these findings, from Work and Pensions Secretary Iain Duncan Smith's think tank, are much less interesting, and arguably far less significant, than a poll of Girl Guides which revealed that fewer than a third believe married couples make better parents than those who are unmarried.

Of the girls and women aged from seven to 21 who were questioned, just 46 per cent see marriage as the gold standard; and just one in five perceives marriage as a 'mark of success' in life.

My first response is not: 'How awful!' Rather it is: 'How in heaven's name was the question worded – and by whom?' One of the Mitfords? The Dowager Countess of Grantham at her snootiest? Not since Lady Edith was jilted at the altar, throwing Downton Abbey into disarray and billowing clouds of gypsophila into the bin, has anyone regarded marriage or the lack thereof as an index of 'success'.

Of the 24 leading universities in the Russell Group, there are just three in which male students are in the majority. Across all UK graduate courses there are 984,000 female students compared with 713,000 males.

So, it is unsurprising that modern girls educated in a system where women dominate law, medicine and veterinary science courses don't regard their big day with dewy-eyed longing; they are too busy focusing on their big careers, and quite rightly so. But when their biological clock starts ticking and children enter the picture, their view of marriage will invariably change. Even if they dare not admit it.

Hand on heart – and here comes the controversy – I do not know of one cohabiting couple with children in which the woman doesn't secretly wish they had got married. There, I've said it.

This is an entirely unscientific view based only on my circle of friends, acquaintances and Kirstie Allsopp, of course, who is given to sighing, in public, about how much she longs to walk down the aisle with her property-developer partner and the father of her children, if only he would ask her.

When discussing the issue with married friends, most couples will say they 'never felt the need' or 'haven't got around to it, yet' or 'don't believe in marriage'. But get her (or, in rarer cases, him) alone and the story is rather different.

'I never thought I would want to get married, but since our son was born, I really do,' says one girlfriend, who runs her own boutique. 'I have suggested it but my boyfriend thinks I'm mad and that it would be a waste of money. I feel I want to consolidate us as a unit.'

Another friend, who is in her sixties and has four adult children, is given to introducing her 'husband' at social occasions with the slightly acid caveat: 'We're not actually married. He was a hippy, so he never asked me. Not that I would want to any more…'

Then there's the friend who frequently cites a nagging feeling of humiliation that kicks in on public transport. 'You see thirtysomething women on the tube with no ring on their finger casting around looking for other women in the same position, and sometimes I have the petty urge to jump up and say: "Don't judge me, I'm not like you, I've got children and a partner,"' she says, with the grace to look shamefaced at the lack of charity in her emotions.

I also know a woman who changed her name by deed poll because her partner refused point blank to marry, but she desperately wanted to have the same surname as her children.

And, finally, I must mention my 40-year-old accountant friend who has always insisted that she is absolutely fine not being married to her partner with whom she has a daughter, son and stepson. She recently phoned me in floods of euphoric tears because he'd presented her with a ruby engagement ring on her milestone birthday.

I'm not recounting any of this as a Bridget Jones-style 'smug married', but because I, too, was rigidly anti-marriage in what would have been my Girl Guiding years. My mother was abruptly widowed a fortnight before my third birthday, when my father died of a heart attack. Brought up in an exclusively female environment – I have four elder sisters – I decided at an early age that men were unreliable because they leave you sad and alone, and I was ever at pains to retain my independence.

But then, in my early thirties, I wanted a baby, so, 11 years into my relationship, I got married. This might sound old-fashioned, clichéd even, but clichés are clichés for a reason.

I don't consider marriage a sign of success, but given that research shows one in three cohabiting couples split up before a child's fifth birthday – compared with one in ten married couples – there's a lot to be said for the stability it confers.

Marriage doesn't guarantee a happy-ever-after any more than a massive white meringue dress vouchsafes the bride's virginity. But it is a signal of intent that, even in this day and age, retains power and meaning.

When Labour leader Ed Miliband married his partner of six years, Justine Thornton, in 2011, many commentators wondered why they'd bothered. After all, they had two children together; was this not a sufficient display of commitment? I thought it very sweet, and even appeared on a television talk show to defend what was apparently a left-field view.

That the pair's children were present at the ceremony exemplified the 21st-century remodelling of marriage. It is an institution whose significance has waxed and waned through history; in the mid-18th century, if a couple cohabited or had children together, they were regarded as being as good as married. It wasn't until the Hardwicke Marriage Act in 1753 that marriage became a legal concept and unmarried couples were stigmatised.

After the boom years of the 1960s and 1970s, when matrimony was a rite of passage, it is now struggling to stay relevant. But following a drop in numbers in recent years, figures show that there were 241,100 marriages in 2010, up by a promising 3.7 per cent.

Obviously, in 2012, there's no longer a social pressure to marry, nor is it necessary for a woman to do it in order to be deemed 'a success'. Those who marry nowadays do so because they want to make a public statement of their commitment. But that commitment is being made later and later – after the job, the house and, yes, the baby.

The average age for a woman's first marriage has climbed from 23.2 in

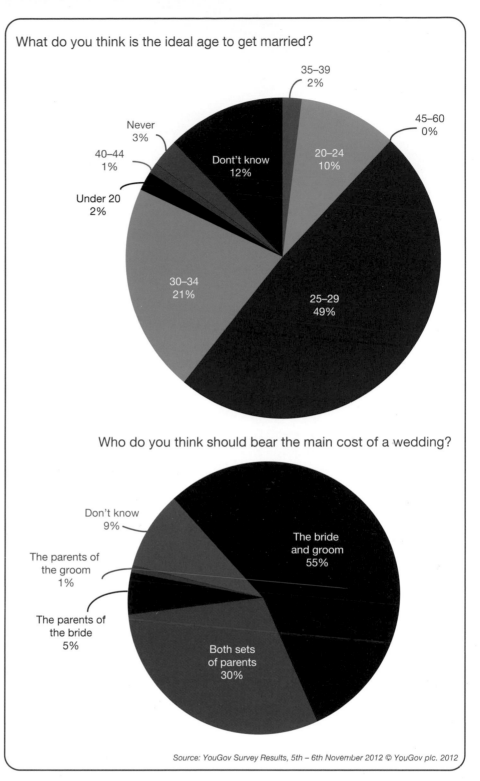

What do you think is the ideal age to get married?

- 35–39: 2%
- 45–60: 0%
- 20–24: 10%
- Never: 3%
- Don't know: 12%
- 40–44: 1%
- Under 20: 2%
- 30–34: 21%
- 25–29: 49%

Who do you think should bear the main cost of a wedding?

- Don't know: 9%
- The parents of the groom: 1%
- The parents of the bride: 5%
- The bride and groom: 55%
- Both sets of parents: 30%

Source: YouGov Survey Results, 5th – 6th November 2012 © YouGov plc. 2012

1981, when Prince Charles married 20-year-old Lady Diana Spencer, to 30 in 2011, when Prince William wed 29-year-old Catherine Middleton.

The latter cohabited before marriage, without so much as a raised eyebrow. Social mores are evolving – but a desire to make a public declaration to a partner, to create officially a family unit, is deep-seated, whatever ardent feminists might say.

For the generation of girls growing up now, feminism is – or ought to be – about choice and opportunity. And

that includes the opportunity to alter the view of marriage they had when they were seven.

9 October 2012

⇨ The above information is reprinted with kind permission from the Telegraph Media Group. Please visit www.telegraph.co.uk for further information.

© *Judith Woods/*
The Daily Telegraph

The myth of common law marriage

The myth of common law marriage – that couples who live together have the same legal rights as married couples – springs from a time when there was uncertainty about what constituted a marriage. Church and State marriage ceremonies are relatively recent – grafted onto older popular rites whose legitimacy was not dependent on written law.

Marriage by consent

In earlier times, the validity of a marriage depended on the consent of the two parties publicly announced or at least symbolised by the exchange of rings or love tokens.

These common rituals were spoken transactions, celebrated by the parties themselves; their witness and memory of the events were the evidence that gave the marriage legitimacy.

Among Anglo-Saxons, the Beweddung was a public ceremony led by the father of the bride. The groom and his people offered weds to the bride's guardians – guarantees that she would be looked after.

In Scotland and the North of England, couples exchanged vows (plighting the troth) by joining their hands in the handfast. He then called her wyf and she called him husband. A woman without a guardian – such as a widow – gave herself to the groom. The partners exchanged weds and rings, kissed and clasped hands, overseen by an orator. The gift by a man to a woman of a ring was popularly believed to imply a formal contract.

Married 'in the eyes of God'

In the 13th century Pope Innocent III declared that the free consent of both spouses, not the formal solemnities by a priest or in church, was the sole essence of a marriage. A valid and binding marriage was created by a verbal contract, performed by an exchange of vows to this effect between a man and a woman over the age of consent (14 and 12), witnessed by two persons, and expressed in the present tense. A promise in the future tense was only binding if it was followed by sexual intercourse which was taken as evidence of consent in the present.

Married 'in the eyes of God and the Church'

Priests became involved, first as orators to invite witnesses and prompt the vows, later offering the church porch as a place to announce and witness vows made at other public places such as the market cross. Gradually the clergy took over the role of orator, asking those attending whether there were objections to the marriage and then getting the couple to repeat publicly their betrothal agreement which was symbolised by rings and coins placed in the priest's book.

By the 1500s most people brought their vows to church as the final part of the marriage process – the first being the betrothal – and a church service started to take place at the altar rather than in the porch. Although the church did not approve of men and women taking themselves as man and wife before their vows were ratified by the church, since canon law recognised this as the basis of holy matrimony, the church courts recognised common rites – spousals, handfasts, and trothplights followed by intercourse – as valid marriages.

Marriage and the law

All three branches of the law – ecclesiastical, common and equity – had control over some aspect of marriage. Medieval canon law determined the rules of marriage, they were revised and restated in the Canons of 1604 and enforced by the church courts. The criminal courts could become involved if either party chose to sue the other for a statutory offence such as bigamy. Equity law had jurisdiction over trust deeds and became involved in marriage where there was litigation concerning marriage settlements and the enforcement of trust deeds. The various courts overlapped and contradictory verdicts as to what was or was not a legally valid marriage could be returned.

After inheritance, marriage was probably the single most important method for the transmission of property. As a result much of the litigation about marriage was litigation about property over which the common law had legal jurisdiction.

Uncertain unions and clandestine marriages

By the 16th century large numbers of people were living together in

situations of varying uncertainty, as there was no consensus about how a legally binding marriage should be conducted. Some – especially the poor – still opted for private verbal contracts, valid in 'the eyes of God', yet often unenforceable in the courts.

Others chose a clandestine marriage conducted by a clergyman following the ritual of the Book of Common Prayer yet violating canon law in a number of ways, most notably by being performed in private without either the reading of banns or a valid licence from a church official. The advantage of such a ceremony was that the involvement of a clergyman gave it respectability and, most importantly, the marriage was recognised as legally binding having full property rights in common law. There was a huge demand for clandestine marriages as they were considerably cheaper than official church marriages and held in secret – an important consideration for minors who feared opposition from parents or servants who feared dismissal.

The state steps in

By the 1730s public opinion was beginning to turn against the clandestine marriage system with complaints in the London newspapers about the fraudulent seduction of heirs and heiresses. In 1753 Lord Harwicke's Marriage Act, 'for the better preventing of clandestine marriages', stipulated that no marriage other than one performed by an ordained Anglican clergyman in the premises of the Church of England after either thrice-called banns or purchase of a licence from bishop or one of his

surrogates was valid. In the case of both banns and licence, at least one party had to be resident for at least three weeks in the parish where the marriage was to be celebrated. Parental consent for those under 21 was strictly enforced. Only the Quakers and Jews managed to have their marriage rites exempted. There were strong objections to the Act – 'proclamations of banns and publick marriages are against the nature and genius of our people' – wrote the *Gentleman's Magazine*.

The continuation of common law marriage practices

Despite the Marriage Act of 1753 ordinary people still tended to keep marriage informal – many felt that the state and the church had no business in their private lives. One informal ceremony was the Gretna Green wedding. The Marriage Act applied to England and Wales, so crossing into Scotland, where you only had to have your consents witnessed, became popular. As the railways opened up, 'package tours' offering bed and breakfast for 'celebration and consummation' were developed. In Yorkshire, Lancashire and Cheshire those who had gone through some kind of common-law rite were said to be 'married on the carpet and the banns up the chimney' or 'married but not churched'.

In almost every part of Britain the term 'living tally' established itself:

They're livin' tally

They've made a tally bargain

They're noant wed, they're nobit livin' tally

While the origins of the term 'tally' are obscure the term became widespread in the 19th century. It conveyed the notion of a definite, if conditional contract or 'bargain', based on the consent of both parties and protecting the women in the case of motherhood. Studies of rural areas have found as many as one in seven couples 'living tally'. In the mid-Victorian period and throughout the following 100 years, common-law arrangements reduced considerably. Since the 1960s a series of administrative rulings, court decisions and laws have given some legal rights to cohabitees, and at the same time the number of couples in cohabiting unions has increased dramatically. These limited rights, however, do not amount to the restoration of the legal recognition of common law marriage, which ceased definitively with the Marriage Act of 1753.

Sources

John R Gillis (1985) For Better For Worse: British Marriages 1600 to the Present. Oxford University Press

Peter Laslett (1979) The World We Have Lost. Methuen

Laurence Stone (1995) Uncertain Unions and Broken Lives. Oxford University Press

⇨ The above information is reprinted with kind permission from OnePlusOne. Please visit www.oneplusone.org.uk for further information.

© OnePlusOne 2009

Distinctive features of marriage

The case for marriage rests in part on the nature of marriage and the processes of relationship formation and maintenance that surround it. It is not simply a couple relationship with a distinct legal status and any evaluation of marriage must include all its features.

⇨ Marriage is a legal relationship that offers protection to its parties in a way that is very hard to replicate by separate agreements. The Law Commission recognises that many people wrongly believe that there is such a concept as 'common law' marriage which offers cohabiting couples similar protection. *http://www. official-documents.gov.uk/ document/cm71/7182/7182.pdf*

⇨ Marriage makes a clear distinction between public and private relationships. Its public nature clarifies third-party obligations: there is no doubt, for example, that a married spouse should receive widow's benefits but there is a grey area around early stage cohabitations. Wider family members have greater clarity about the nature and status of the relationship.

⇨ Marriage is an intentional act of commitment. Cohabiting couples can slide into parental responsibilities or shared financial commitments without making a decision about their commitment to each other. These responsibilities create inertia in the relationship: relationships continue which might otherwise have ended earlier but without the mutual commitment that can help in pressured circumstances. The intentional commitment of marriage is known to be a protective factor. (Rhoades, Stanley and Markman (2006) Pre-engagement commitment and gender asymmetry in marital commitment)

⇨ Marriage also provides a natural trigger point to access relationships education in a way that cohabitation does not (although the birth of a child is another important trigger point).

⇨ The nature of marriage as a social institution brings with it a range of social norms which can promote behaviours more likely to safeguard the relationship.

Positive benefits of marriage

⇨ Higher incomes and greater accumulation of wealth (and avoiding the loss of income that tends to follow the breakdown of relationships) See, for example, Zagorsky, Marriage and Divorce's Impact on Wealth *http:// jos.sagepub.com/ content/41/4/406.short*

⇨ Improved health and wellbeing. One study suggests that 'the size of the health gain from marriage is remarkable – it may be as large as the benefit from giving up smoking' *www2.warwick.ac.uk/fac/soc/ economics/staff/academic/ oswald/healthlong2005.pdf*

⇨ Cohabiting people are significantly less happy in their relationships than married people, and children are happier when growing up with both biological parents (Understanding Society survey, ONS)

⇨ A typical finding of cross-national studies is that 'much can be done to improve child wellbeing through economic and other supports where the institution of marriage has seriously weakened and cohabitation has become common. But even in nations that have the most extensive welfare measures, such as the Scandinavian countries and France, a substantial gap in child wellbeing remains between those children who grow up in intact families, and those who do not... all the evidence we have shows that individuals fare best, both in childhood and in later life, when they benefit from the economic and emotional investments of their natural parents who reside together continuously and cooperate in raising them.' *Popenoe, D. 2009. Social Science and Public Policy. Vol 46, Number 5, pp. 429–436. http://www.springerlink.com/ content/h155411803161mv5/*

⇨ The above information is reprinted with kind permission from The Marriage Foundation. Please visit www. marriagefoundation.org.uk for further information.

© The Marriage Foundation 2013

Is pro-marriage campaign on firm foundations?

By Vicki McLynn, Partner, Pannone Solicitors

The number of marriages in England and Wales has been in almost constant decline for the past four decades, so recent figures showing that there had been a slight rebound were the cause for genuine cheer among its proponents.

According to the Office of National Statistics, 3.7% more couples headed up the aisle in 2010 than had the previous year.

However, it hasn't all been untrammelled (wedded) bliss. The year in question followed a 12-month period which had witnessed fewer couples getting married than at any stage since 1895.

If that wasn't bad enough, the figures emerged only months after the ONS released yet more data showing that divorce also enjoyed something of a revival in 2010, up 4.9% on the year before.

It is against that backdrop that a fresh initiative has been launched to revitalise the fortunes of matrimony. High Court judge, Sir Paul Coleridge, has set up The Marriage Foundation to, as he puts it, end the 'destructive scourge' of divorce.

His campaign is in part, he maintains, a reaction to the almost casual nature of celebrity relationships devoured by the nation's gossip magazines.

Backed by other experts on Family law from among his fellow justices and academia, Sir Paul seeks to make marriage the 'gold standard' for relationships. His aim is to reduce relationship breakdowns which exact such an emotional toll both on parents and the estimated 3.8 million children who he says are caught up each year in the family justice system.

Sir Paul hopes the initiative will also hopefully cut the annual financial cost of break-ups – which he puts at £42 billion – into the bargain.

The Foundation is being launched in London's Middle Temple Hall, one of the capital's four ancient Inns of Court, and will attempt to influence the way people regard marriage and the choices they make about the relationships they forge. Information on marriage will be provided via a variety of sources with a particular emphasis on the Internet.

The material will underline how marriage amounts to far more than a vow, a cake and a piece of paper as well as highlighting the nature of support available for those husbands and wives whose relationships run into difficulties.

Given the fundamental intention of Sir Paul's campaign, it might seem difficult or truculent to take issue. I and my colleagues also see the damage and distress wrought by relationship breakdown.

Any attempts to address and undo the often lasting impact which it has are to be rightly applauded. It is impossible, though, not to have some reservations at least with the narrow focus of the Foundation.

I would argue that there's a real need to support relationships of whatever kind. It is a point to which Sir Paul alludes when he highlights how other agencies may support relationships of all types – something which is, he says, 'valuable work but not our mission'.

Critics might suggest that it is wrong to rank one solid, stable environment as being better than another just as it is to imply that individuals enter into divorce as lightly as certain high-profile figures are alleged to do.

Few, if any, people make the decision to separate on a whim. My own experience is reflected in those of other Family lawyers at Pannone and many of our peers. Those people who come to us for initial advice about divorce have generally only taken that step after great consideration.

The noble sentiments which lie behind the Marriage Foundation's own foundation also appear to be a bold attempt to reverse recent trends. A third of marriages which do take place in England and Wales don't last 15 years. Even the ONS data which trumpeted an increase in marriages showed a rise in the number of people who were remarrying after bereavement or divorce.

And there's no guaranteed lasting comfort in a second or third betrothal. One-fifth of all those people getting divorced had, according to the most recent figures, been divorced before.

Add to that an increase in the proportion of people, both old and young, choosing to live together without marrying and it is clear that society's view of marriage is radically different to what it was when Sir Paul became a barrister in 1970.

That shouldn't, of course, be seen as devaluing what he is trying to do. Any measures which can highlight the importance of stable family life – and the consequences of its erosion for the partners and their dependents – are worthwhile.

Trying to distinguish between the respective merits of cohabitation or marriage, rather than accepting that each has its own benefits, carries with it the risk of creating disharmony – the very thing which Sir Paul is creditably trying to avoid.

1 May 2012

⇨ The above information is reprinted with kind permission from *The Huffington Post*. Please visit www.huffingtonpost.co.uk for further information.

Facts about forced marriage

What is forced marriage?

A forced marriage occurs when one or both spouses do not (or, in the case of children and some adults at risk, cannot) consent to the marriage and duress is involved. Duress can include physical, psychological, financial, sexual and emotional pressure, threatening conduct, harassment, threat of blackmail, use of deception and other means. It is also force to knowingly take advantage of a person's incapacity to consent to, or understand the nature of, the marriage.

The Scottish and UK Governments regard forced marriage as a form of domestic abuse, an abuse of human rights and, when children and young people are affected, child abuse.

There is a direct link between forced marriage and crimes committed in the name of 'honour'. The most extreme examples – 'honour' killings – are committed in the belief that defiled honour can only be redeemed when the source of shame, that is the victim, is removed. This is often done in collusion with relatives and the community.

The difference between forced and arranged marriage

Forced marriage is different from arranged marriage. In an arranged marriage, the families of both spouses take a leading role in arranging the marriage but the choice whether or not to accept the arrangement remains with the prospective spouses.

In forced marriage, one or both spouses do not (or, in the case of children and some adults at risk, cannot) consent to the marriage and duress is involved.

If families have to resort to violence or emotional pressure to make someone marry, that person's consent has not been given freely and, therefore, it is a forced marriage.

Who is affected?

Both men and women are forced into marriage although most cases involve women aged between 13 and 30. However, there is no 'typical' victim of forced marriage.

Forced marriage is not limited to first marriages and can affect those who are widowed or divorced.

Of 1,735 contacts to the Forced Marriage Unit in 2010, 14 per cent involved a male victim and 86 per cent a female victim.

Lesbian, gay, bisexual or transgender (LGBT) people are also victims of forced marriage. Of the above contacts, there were 36 instances which involved victims who identified themselves as LGBT.

Of the above contacts, 70 involved people with disabilities (50 with learning disabilities, 17 with physical disabilities and three with both). Evidence suggests that for people with learning disabilities, forced marriage may occur at a similar rate for men and women. Research also indicates that the forced marriage of people with learning disabilities is likely to be significantly under-reported and can differ from the way in which forced marriage presents generally. Most reported cases in the UK so far have involved South Asian families (Pakistani, Indian and Bangladeshi). This partly reflects the fact that there is a large, established South Asian population here. However, there have been cases involving East Asian, Middle Eastern, European and African communities.

Forced marriage is not associated with particular religions or religious practice and has been recorded in Christian, Jewish, Hindu, Muslim and Sikh communities.

Some forced marriages take place in Scotland with no overseas

Case study

E was born in the UK but her parents were from Somalia. She was at university and things were not going well at home because her parents thought she was becoming too 'westernised' and disapproved of her smoking and drinking and having a boyfriend. Her mother tricked her, saying that she wanted to take E on holiday to Somalia to show her where she and E's father had grown up. When they arrived, she was chained to a wall of the house in which they were staying until she was forced to marry a much older man. E tried to run away. Her mother called the police and the police arrested E and put her in a prison where there were other women who had resisted marriage. After being let out of prison, E pretended to capitulate. She was allowed to go into the local town where she managed to email a friend in the UK. The friend contacted the Forced Marriage Unit. The FMU managed to arrange to have her smuggled out of Somalia to Ethiopia and onto a plane home where she went into refuge. She was very frightened because she had 'brought shame' on her family by running away and feared that if her family found her, they would kill her.

element, while others involve a partner coming here from overseas or a British national being sent abroad.

> **"My family were shocked and very angry when they found out I was gay. They were violent towards me and called me names. My mother tried to calm things but couldn't. I felt guilty that I had caused them pain and let them down. They made me feel as if I owed them. They really believed that if I married who they wanted, I would stop being gay"**

Some cases are immigration-related with victims forced to marry family members in order to facilitate their entry to the UK.

Prevalence of forced marriage

Many cases of forced marriage, as with domestic abuse generally, go unreported. Many of the families involved do not consider the marriage as 'forced' and many victims are unwilling to speak out. With greater awareness of the help available, the number of cases reported is likely to increase.

The Forced Marriage Unit deals with around 400 cases of forced marriage a year (469 cases in 2010). Until 2009, approximately ten per cent involved people from Scotland. In 2010, this percentage was significantly less at 2.7 per cent. The likely reason for this is that Scottish victims are now seeking advice and support from organisations in Scotland.

The main support organisations for female victims in Scotland are Shakti Women's Aid in Edinburgh and Hemat Gryffe Women's Aid in Glasgow. In 2010–11 Shakti Women's Aid supported 12 forced marriage cases and Hemat Gryffe Women's Aid 13 cases.

There is no reliable source of information which captures the cases involving male victims of forced marriage in Scotland.

Case study

Born and brought up in Scotland, M was 16 when she approached Women's Aid asking for information on domestic abuse 'for a friend'. She came back the next day asking to speak to the same worker and said that her family were forcing her to marry her cousin, also 16. The family planned to visit their home country in the summer holidays and get her married. Her father was abusing her because of her refusal to cooperate and was threatening to stop her from going to school.

Women's Aid helped M plan her escape from home and go to a refuge in another city. It was difficult for her to leave her mother and siblings. She was extremely protective of them, felt guilty about leaving them and worried about them. She was concerned that domestic abuse against her mother by the extended family would increase. So, after a few days in hiding, she phoned her mother who pressured her to meet. Her mother told her:

⇨ 'Your granddad had a heart attack and is in the hospital and wants to see you.'

⇨ 'Your sisters and brothers are very upset and not eating.'

⇨ 'If you come back, we will move out of Edinburgh, and leave your dad.'

⇨ 'We can't face the community so we are leaving the UK.'

Despite intense pressure, M was resolute. Eventually, her mother and siblings returned overseas but phoned constantly asking her to join them. Her mother insisted that M should visit for a short while, 'for the family's honour', and that they would not force her to marry. M finally gave in and left Scotland to meet her mother. She later returned to Scotland with a husband. Her two sisters stayed overseas because

the family did not want them to refuse to marry as M had done. Both were engaged to their cousins by the time they were 13.

Motives for forced marriage

Perpetrators of forced marriage often justify the practice as protecting their daughters/sons, building stronger families and preserving cultural or religious traditions. They often do not see anything wrong in their actions. They may believe that they are upholding the cultural traditions of their home country although practices and values there may have changed. For adults with support needs, including learning disabilities, families may believe it is the right or only option to secure continuing personal care for that person and may be very open about their intentions.

Some parents come under significant pressure from their extended families to have their daughters/sons married.

Sometimes a marriage agreement is made when a child is an infant. They may go through their entire

> **"People don't realise that men can also find themselves in this situation. I don't know if I could have told anyone even if I'd had the chance to. It's not exactly macho, is it, admitting that you were held hostage by your family and forced to marry someone you'd never met..."**

childhood expecting to marry someone their parents select. They may not know that they have a fundamental human right to choose their own partner. However, they may also be completely unaware, until the marriage is imminent or actually taking place, that they have already been 'promised' in marriage to a complete stranger, or relative, whom they have little or no knowledge about and may never have met.

Motives include:

⇨ Controlling unwanted behaviour, sexuality, sexual orientation or gender identity (including perceived promiscuity, or being LGBT – particularly the behaviour and sexuality of women

⇨ Controlling unwanted behaviour, for example, alcohol and drug use, socialising unchaperoned with, or simply speaking to, members of the opposite sex who are not family members, wearing make-up or behaving in what is perceived to be a 'westernised' manner

⇨ Preventing 'unsuitable' relationships, for example, outside the ethnic, cultural, religious or caste group

⇨ Protecting 'family honour' or 'izzat' (for example this might be related to a victim disclosing rape or sexual abuse)

⇨ Responding to peer group or family pressure about conforming to expectations

⇨ Attempting to strengthen family links

⇨ Financial gain or obtaining financial security for a person with a learning disability

⇨ Ensuring land, property and wealth remain within the family

⇨ Protecting perceived cultural ideals

⇨ Protecting perceived religious ideals

⇨ Ensuring care for someone with learning/physical disability when parents or existing carers are unable to fulfil that role or because of mistrust of external social care

⇨ Concerns that younger siblings may be seen as undesirable if older sons or daughters are not already married – this could include marrying off a young person with learning/physical disability because their unmarried status might be seen as a barrier to marriage for their siblings

⇨ Assisting claims for UK residence and citizenship

⇨ Obtaining physical assistance or personal care for ageing parents.

"I've always wanted to be independent, so I only agreed to go because they said my grandma was sick. It wasn't true; when I got there they showed me new clothes and jewellery and said the wedding would be at the end of the week. They knew I'd be isolated when I got there because I am deaf"

There are no excuses

While it is important to be aware of the motives which drive some people to perpetrate forced marriage, you should not accept them as justification. Forced marriage is a violation of children's rights under the UN Convention on the Rights of the Child as well as a form of violence against women and an abuse of human rights under the Universal Declaration on Human Rights.

There is no justification for forced marriage or for practitioners not acting to prevent it. You may be concerned about cultural sensitivity. But such concerns do not excuse failure to assist victims or to take action (safely) if you suspect that someone is forcing or has forced another into marriage.

Forced marriage cannot be justified on religious grounds: every major faith condemns it and freely given consent in marriage is a prerequisite of all religions.

⇨ The above information is reprinted with kind permission from The Scottish Government. Please visit www.scotland.gov.uk for further information.

© Crown Copyright 2013

Child marriage: a global problem

Millions of young women around the world are married before they turn 18, many against their will and in violation of international laws and conventions on women's rights. These young brides have limited education and economic opportunities, and they are vulnerable to health complications that result from giving birth before their bodies are fully developed. They often are socially isolated and powerless in the relationship. Ending child marriage can help nations and communities meet goals related to poverty, education, gender equality, maternal and child health, and HIV/AIDS.

Global problem

⇨ Over the last decade, 58 million young women – one in three – in developing countries have been married before the age of 18.

⇨ One in nine girls – or 15 million – in these countries was married by 15.

⇨ The highest rates of marriage before 18 (generally considered to be child marriage) are found in Africa. In Niger, 75 per cent of girls marry before 18; in Chad, 72 per cent; and in Mali, 71 per cent.

⇨ New data on marriage of young adolescents shows that in Nepal, seven per cent of girls are married by age ten, and 40 per cent by age 15. In Mali, Bangladesh, and parts of India, one in five girls is married by 15.

Health and social consequences

⇨ Childbirth complications are the leading cause of death for girls ages 15 to 19 in developing countries.

⇨ Girls whose bodies have not fully developed are at greater risk for obstetric fistula, a debilitating medical condition often caused by prolonged or obstructed labour.

⇨ Infants born to teenage mothers are more likely to suffer low birth weight and premature birth and are more likely to die. Children of young mothers also are more likely to be malnourished.

⇨ Studies have shown that marrying young increases a girl's chance of acquiring HIV. Often, her husband is much older and more sexually experienced, which makes him more likely to be infected. Married girls also have frequent sex and have little ability to negotiate condom use or abstinence.

⇨ Girls who marry young often drop out of school, which leaves them with few income-producing skills – a loss with grave consequences for them and their future families, as women who earn incomes usually invest in their families and children.

⇨ Studies show education has a protective effect on women: literate women are more likely to know basic facts about HIV and their children are more likely to survive past the age of five.

Laws, culture and social norms

⇨ Nearly three-quarters of countries have laws that set the minimum age for girls to marry at 18 or older, but often such laws are not enforced. Also many of the laws have exceptions, such as allowing early marriage with parental consent.

⇨ Nearly one-third of nations set a younger minimum age for girls to marry than for boys.

⇨ Social and economic realities, such as money and goods that must be paid to a girl's parents, and cultural and religious traditions help to perpetuate child marriage.

⇨ Studies have shown that women with less education tend to marry at a younger age.

⇨ A UNICEF study found that Tanzanian women with secondary education were 92 per cent less likely to be married before they were 18 than were women who attended only primary school.

Promising approaches

⇨ In rural Ethiopia, a project targeting young women provided mentoring from adult women in the community, economic incentives to remain in school, and improved access to reproductive health information and services. Early marriage among participants dropped significantly.

⇨ Senegal's Tostan community empowerment project reduced early marriage through sessions on human rights, democracy, and health that included education on the right to free consent to marriage and the health problems that child marriage and early childbearing can cause.

⇨ In Bangladesh, scholarships for secondary school proved to greatly influence parents' decisions to keep their daughters in school. The scholarships increased girls' enrolment and attendance significantly.

⇨ A project in Nepal focused on providing income-generating skills to young girls to help support themselves financially, stay in school, and avoid early marriage.

⇨ The above information is reprinted with kind permission from the Population Reference Bureau (PRB). Please visit www.prb.org for further information.

© Population Reference Bureau 2013

What is civil partnership?

Civil partners have equal treatment to married couples in a wide range of legal matters.

Who can register?

⇨ Two people may register a civil partnership provided they are of the same sex;

⇨ They are not already in a civil partnership or lawfully married;

⇨ They are not within prohibited degrees of relationship (e.g. closely related);

⇨ They are both aged 16 or over (and, if either of them is under 18, the consent of the appropriate person has been obtained).

What happens at a civil partnership registration?

A civil partnership is registered once the couple have signed the civil partnership document (the schedule) in the presence of a registrar and two witnesses.

There are words printed on the document which the couple will be able to say at the time of signing the document, but the couple are not legally required to say any words – there is therefore no prescribed ceremony that you have to go through – it is the signing of the schedule which makes the process legally recognised.

What time of day can a civil partnership be registered?

Civil partnerships can be registered at any time with the prior agreement of the registration authority, the date and time being arranged with the registration authority.

Can we have a ceremony?

Yes, you can arrange a ceremony in addition to the signing of the legal documentation if you wish, but a ceremony is not required under the Act. It is up to you to decide. Cornwall Registration Service has developed a number of beautiful ceremonies for you to choose from. The ceremony can be a very simple one with just a few words spoken or something more elaborate.

Where can civil partnership registration take place?

Civil partnership registration can take place at a Registration Office, approved venue or any religious premise approved as a venue for civil partnerships. In Cornwall we have a wide range of exciting venues that have been approved for civil partnership registration. The venues have been approved for civil partnership and marriage. Approved venues are legally able to allow the conduct of civil marriage, or civil partnership, or both on their premises.

How does civil partnership differ from marriage?

Civil partnership is a legal relationship exclusively for same-sex couples distinct from marriage. The Government has sought to give civil partners parity of treatment with spouses, as far as is possible, in the rights and responsibilities that flow from forming a civil partnership.

There are a small number of differences between civil partnership and marriage, for example, a civil partnership is formed when the second civil partner signs the relevant document. A civil marriage is formed when the couple exchanges spoken words. Opposite-sex couples can opt for a religious or civil marriage ceremony, whereas formation of a civil partnership will be an exclusively civil procedure although it may take place within a religious premise approved for civil partnership registration.

⇨ The above information is reprinted with kind permission from Cornwall Council. Please visit www.cornwall.gov.uk for further information.

© Cornwall Council 2013

You're gay, you're in love, you want to be together forever... get hitched!

A guide to civil partnership.

So, civil partnership, is this marriage or not?

To all intents and purposes, yes. With civil partnerships you get every right and every privilege – and every responsibility – straight couples get when they marry.

It's the same thing. You can even ask your relations for toasters.

What sort of rights do you mean?

Apart from the right to a new toaster and a great party? You get next-of-kin rights, you get rights in relation to your partner's children, you get tax rights, including the same inheritance rights as straight married couples. And you get pension rights, so you may be able to claim your civil partner's pension should they die…

Is that what we become, civil partners?

Yeah, but no one can stop you calling each other what you like – husband, wife, husbear, her indoors – though not on official documents. If you want to take your partner's name on your driver's licence say, or your passport, proof of identity and your civil partnership certificate will be enough to sort that out.

So, there's no inheritance tax between partners any more?

No, because you are now civil partners and recognised like a straight married couple. You have the right to register a death, the right to bereavement benefits, the right to claim compensation in case of a fatal accident, the right to stay living in your shared rented home…

But we don't have to live together to be civil partners?

No. It's the same for married straight couples. Domestic arrangements and who lives where are nobody else's business. And your bosses do have to treat you and your civil partner the same way they treat a married straight couple in terms of perks and benefits.

You said there were also responsibilities…

Well, it's legally binding so it's not something to do for a laugh or a quick romantic gesture. You'll have to live with the consequences, including maybe providing maintenance to your civil partner and any children. And if you're receiving benefits, you will be dealt with the same as any other married couple. But then that's true of all couples – straight or gay – just living together without the piece of paper.

So, presumably, we'd have to get a divorce if it all went wrong?

It's called a 'dissolution' but yes, you would.

And we can tie the knot in church?

You can have a blessing in a church with your favourite gay-friendly vicar (or equivalent gay-friendly religious leader), the same as straight couples who marry in a register office, but there can be no religious service during the registration itself, just as with straight couples in a civil wedding. But that doesn't mean you can't get spliced somewhere beautiful. You can do the deed anywhere that has a licence for civil services – stately homes, hotels, selected beaches and mountain tops.

What happens when we're being registered?

It's your day. You can have what you want, so don't let any officials bully you into something you're not up for – or out of something you are! You can write your own vows, exchange rings, have whatever readings you like, kiss to seal the deal, whatever – just discuss it all with your registrar. The only thing you absolutely have to do is provide your signatures and two witnesses.

And does this count with the Immigration Office?

Yes, you'll now be in exactly the same boat as straight couples who get married. There may be restrictions about entering the country to register but no more than there would be for a straight partner.

So, how do we get started?

You need to go to the registration service – in person – to give formal notice of your intention to register your partnership, just as a straight couple would. And remember, you don't have to tie the knot locally – you can go anywhere you like In the UK as long as it has a licence. Once you've given notice, you have 15 days to wait, plan, choose outfits, invite friends and make a fool of yourself on a stag or hen night.

For everything you need to know about civil partnerships go to:

⇨ www.stonewall.org.uk

⇨ www.stonewallcymru.org.uk

⇨ The above information is reprinted with kind permission from Stonewall and Warwick Worldwide. Please visit www.stonewall.org.uk for further information.

© Stonewall 2013

couples. This rule can be over-ridden by contrary provisions in the Bill where necessary.

Part 2 – Other provisions relating to marriage and civil partnership

Clause 12 with Schedule 5 enables a person in a marriage with someone of the opposite sex to preserve their marriage (if they both wish) when one of them changes their legal gender.

Clause 13 with Schedule 6 enables same sex couples to get married in overseas consulates and on armed forces bases overseas.

Part 3 – Final provisions

Clause 14 with Schedule 7 gives the Secretary of State powers to make orders facilitating the transition between the current arrangements and the new arrangements.

Clause 15 sets out the powers to make secondary legislation which have been delegated to Ministers, along with the parliamentary procedures when certain powers are exercised.

Clause 16 sets outs how certain terms used in the Bill are to be interpreted.

Clause 17 sets out the territorial extent and application of the Bill's provisions. Generally, the Bill affects England and Wales only, except for certain circumstances when it affects Scotland and Northern Ireland.

Clause 18 gives the Bill's title and enables it to be brought into force by Orders made by the Secretary of State.

More detail on the Bill can be found in the Explanatory Notes on the parliamentary website http://www.parliament.uk/business/bills-and-legislation/

⇨ The above information is reprinted with kind permission from the Government Equalities Office. Please visit www.gov.uk for further information.

Same Sex Marriage Bill storms through House of Commons

'Truly historic step forward' passed by 400 to 175 votes.

MPs have voted by a majority of 225 in favour of the new Marriage (Same Sex Couples) Bill. The Bill will extend the legal form of marriage to lesbian, gay and bisexual people and permit religious denominations to celebrate such marriages should they wish.

Stonewall Chief Executive Ben Summerskill said: 'As the last piece of the legislative jigsaw providing equality for gay people in Britain, this is a truly historic step forward. We're absolutely delighted that MPs have demonstrated so overwhelmingly that they're in touch with the twenty-first century.

'We anticipate, as always, a tough battle in the House of Lords. Happily, the size of the Commons majority seen tonight – much larger than for most normal Government business – will make it very difficult for peers to suggest that the Bill should be rejected.

'Most people in Britain support equal marriage and will be delighted that we're now a step closer to it. We're grateful to the thousands of Stonewall supporters, many of them straight, who played a big part by contacting their MPs in support.'

The Marriage (Same Sex Couples) Bill will now go into Commons Committee Stage and is likely to progress to the House of Lords after the Queen's Speech, expected in early May.

YouGov polling for Stonewall shows that 71% of people in Britain support equal marriage. This figure rises to 82% of those under the age of 50. To find out more about Stonewall's campaign for equal marriage, visit www.stonewall.org.uk/marriage.

5 February 2013

⇨ The above information is reprinted with kind permission from Stonewall. Please visit www.stonewall.org.uk for further information.

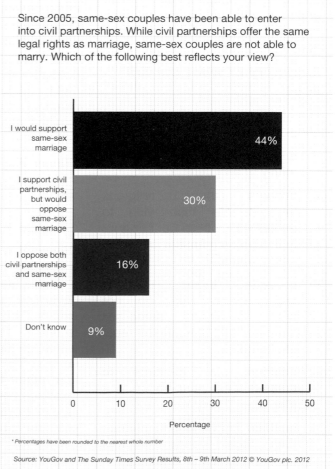

Since 2005, same-sex couples have been able to enter into civil partnerships. While civil partnerships offer the same legal rights as marriage, same-sex couples are not able to marry. Which of the following best reflects your view?

	Percentage
I would support same-sex marriage	44%
I support civil partnerships, but would oppose same-sex marriage	30%
I oppose both civil partnerships and same-sex marriage	16%
Don't know	9%

* Percentages have been rounded to the nearest whole number

Source: YouGov and The Sunday Times Survey Results, 8th – 9th March 2012 © YouGov plc. 2012

Ten reasons why the Government is wrong to redefine marriage

Reason 1

It will undermine marriage

Evidence shows that redefining marriage actually undermines support for marriage in wider society. Neither has it delivered the promised stability for same-sex couples. In Spain, after gay marriage was introduced, marriage rates across the whole population plummeted.[1] In The Netherlands too there has been a significant fall in the marriage rate since marriage was redefined.[2] Same-sex marriage does not promote marriage.

Reason 2

Marriage is part of our history

Marriage between a man and a woman is not a recent social invention. Everyone knows that marriage predates law, nation and church. It goes back to the dawn of time. Yes, matrimonial law may have been tweaked over the years, but the law has never fundamentally altered the essential nature of marriage: a lifelong commitment between one man and one woman. Same-sex marriage would rewrite hundreds of years of British legal tradition and thousands of years of cultural heritage.

Reason 3

Equality already exists

Same-sex couples already have equality. All the legal rights of marriage are already available to same-sex couples through civil partnerships. Equality doesn't mean bland uniformity or state-imposed sameness. If the Government genuinely wants to pursue equality, why is it banning heterosexual couples from entering a civil partnership? Same-sex couples have equal rights through civil partnerships, but they don't have the right to redefine marriage for everyone else.

Reason 4

Impact on schools

The current law requires schools to teach children about the importance of marriage. If marriage is given a new definition, it will be endorsed in schools. According to expert legal advice, any teacher who fails to endorse same-sex marriage in the classroom could be dismissed. Parents will have no legal right to withdraw their children from lessons which endorse same-sex marriage across the curriculum. Already supporters of gay marriage are recommending books for use in schools which undermine traditional marriage, and call on schools to get children to act out gay weddings.[3] The effect on schools will be polarising and divisive.

> **"Rewriting the meaning of marriage will have a far-reaching impact on society"**

Reason 5

Thin end of the wedge

If we redefine marriage once, what's to stop marriage being redefined yet further? If marriage is solely about love and commitment between consenting adults, what's to say we shouldn't recognise three-way relationships? It's already happened in nations that redefined marriage. In Brazil, a three-way relationship was given marriage-like recognition under civil partnership laws.[4] A similar situation has existed in The

3 Stonewall Education Guides, Including different families, Stonewall, pages 11-13

4 The Daily Telegraph, 28 August 2012

1 Instituto Nacional de Estadística, Press Release, Vital Statistics and Basic Demographic Indicators: Preview data for 2011, 29 June 2012, page 5

2 Duncan, William C, 'The Tenth Anniversary of Dutch Same-Sex Marriage: How Is Marriage Doing in the Netherlands?', iMAPP Research Brief, Vol.4, No.3, 2011; Marriages and Partnership registrations: Key Statistics, CBSStatLine, 2012, see http://tinyurl.com/colyp2o

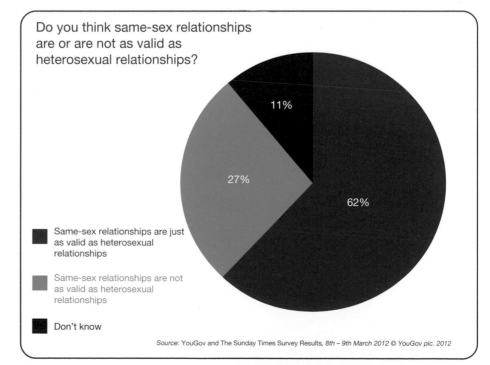

Do you think same-sex relationships are or are not as valid as heterosexual relationships?

- 11%
- 27%
- 62%

■ Same-sex relationships are just as valid as heterosexual relationships

■ Same-sex relationships are not as valid as heterosexual relationships

■ Don't know

Source: YouGov and The Sunday Times Survey Results, 8th – 9th March 2012 © YouGov plc. 2012

Netherlands for several years.[5] In Canada after marriage was redefined, a polygamist argued in court that his relationship should be recognised in law.[6] When politicians meddle with marriage it all starts to unravel.

Reason 6
Marginalises the majority

Calling opponents 'bigots' is meant to shut down debate and stop people thinking for themselves. Nick Clegg landed in hot water over a draft speech which called opponents of redefining marriage 'bigots'.[7] He later retracted the word, but there's no doubt that many who support this radical agenda think anyone who disagrees is not worthy of respect. However, support for traditional marriage has come from many respected academics, lawyers, politicians of all parties, and religious leaders. They all know that redefining marriage would have a profound impact.

"Seven in ten people want to keep marriage as it is"

Reason 7
Many gay people don't want it

Polling shows that only a minority of gay people (39 per cent) believe gay marriage is a priority.[8] And according to the Government only three per cent of gay people would enter a

same-sex marriage.[9] A number of gay celebrities and journalists are themselves opposed to gay marriage. Latest official data shows that only 0.5 per cent of households are headed by a same-sex couple.[10] Not all of them want, or will enter, a same-sex marriage. So, why is such a monumental change being imposed throughout society?

Reason 8
The public don't want it

Seven in ten people want to keep marriage as it is.[11] Other polling which purports to show public support for gay marriage fails to tell respondents that equal rights are already available through civil partnerships.[12] When people are told this crucial fact, most people say keep marriage as it is.[13] MPs say their postbags have been dominated by public opposition to redefining marriage.[14] Ordinary people want the Government to concentrate on reviving the economy and providing better public services, not meddling with marriage.[15]

Reason 9
A huge change to society

Since we already have civil partnerships, isn't same-sex marriage just a small logical next step? No. Rewriting the meaning of marriage will

have a far-reaching impact on society. Over 3,000 laws make reference to marriage. The Government has already admitted that official documents will need to be rewritten to remove words like 'husband' and 'wife'. In France the Government is eradicating the words 'father' and 'mother' from all official documents. The Church of England has warned that it could lead to disestablishment and a constitutional crisis.[16]

Reason 10
Freedom of conscience will be eroded

The civil liberty of people who believe in traditional marriage is already being eroded. A housing manager from Manchester was demoted and lost 40 per cent of his salary for stating, outside work time, that gay weddings in churches were 'an equality too far'.[17] Conferences and symposiums in support of traditional marriage have been thrown out of venues. Adverts in support of a 600,000-strong public petition in favour of traditional marriage have been investigated as 'offensive'.[18] And all this has taken place before any change to the law has taken place. What will it be like if the law does change? A leading human rights lawyer has outlined the devastating impact of redefining marriage on civil liberties.[19]

⇨ The above information is reprinted with kind permission from the Coalition for Marriage. Please visit c4m.org.uk for further information.

© Coalition for Marriage 2013

5 The Brussels Journal, 26 September 2005, see http://www.brusselsjournal.com/node/301; This was an example of a cohabitation agreement [Government of the Netherlands, Marriage, Registered Partnership and Cohabitation Agreements, see http://tinyurl.com/bdykz59]

6 PinkNews.co.uk, 4 February 2009, see http://www.pinknews.co.uk/2009/02/04/mormon-accused-ofpolygamy-to-use-gay-marriage-as-defence/

7 The Daily Mail, 12 September 2012

8 39 per cent of respondents identifying as gay/lesbian/bisexual or other agreed with the statement 'I think redefining marriage is a priority for gay people'. 27 per cent disagreed, 34 per cent said 'don't know'. See Civil Partnerships Survey, ComRes, 27 April - 20 May 2012, Table 3, page 12

9 The Government's 'best estimate assumes no increase in demand' for same-sex marriage, over and above the current demand for civil partnerships as they have 'no evidence that there would be such an increase' [Equal civil marriage consultation Impact Assessment, Government Equalities Office, January 2012, pages 2 and 5]. Around 3 per cent of homosexuals have ever been in a civil partnership (based on ONS figures of civil partnership registration and using the Government's estimate that 6 per cent of the population are LGB)

10 Families and Households, 2012, Office for National Statistics, 1 November 2012, Table 1, page 4

11 Marriage Survey, ComRes, 23-24 February 2012, Table 1, page 2

12 Gay Couples' Rights Survey, Populus, 9-11 March 2012, Table 2, page 2; Sunday Telegraph Survey, ICM, 7-8 March 2012, Table 1, page 1

13 Sunday Times Survey, YouGov, 8-9 March 2012, page 7; Marriage Attitude Survey, ComRes, 6-8 January 2012

14 The Daily Telegraph, 1 October 2012

15 Sunday Telegraph Survey, ICM, 7-8 March 2012, Table 4, page 7; The Sunday Telegraph, 11 March 2012

16 The Daily Telegraph, 14 March 2012; Equal Civil Marriage – Impact Assessment, Home Office, January 2012, pages 7-8; Mail Online, 24 September 2012, see http://tinyurl.com/9trjds8; Telegraph.co.uk, 12 June 2012, see http://tinyurl.com/7h4mp3w

17 The Mail on Sunday, 23 October 2011

18 Mail Online, 15 May 2012, see http://tinyurl.com/b3jdx8n

19 Re: The Implications for Freedom of Conscience and Religious Liberty Arising from Redefining Marriage in England and Wales, Aidan O'Neill, 27 July 2012. See summary at http://c4m.org.uk/downloads/legalopinionsummary.pdf

Same-sex marriage: mythbuster

Setting out the truth.

MYTH: Allowing same-sex couples to marry will destroy the institution of marriage.

REALITY: Marriage is a hugely important institution in this country. The principles of long-term commitment and responsibility which underpin it bind society together and make it stronger. The Government believes that we should not prevent people getting married unless there are very good reasons – and loving someone of the same sex is not one of them.

MYTH: Marriage has not changed in hundreds of years.

REALITY: Marriage is not static. It has always been an evolving institution. In the 19th century inequalities prevented Catholics, atheists, Baptists and many others from marrying except in the Anglican Church. In the 20th century the law was changed to recognise married men and married women as equal before law. Opening up marriage to all couples will strengthen the vital institution of marriage, and help ensure that it remains an essential building block of society.

MYTH: Religious organisations or minister of religion will be forced to conduct same-sex marriages.

REALITY: This is not true. The Marriage (Same Sex Couples) Bill makes clear that no religious organisation or religious minister will be compelled to marry same-sex couples. A 'quadruple lock' of legal protections will ensure that all religious organisations are free to choose and can act according to their doctrines and beliefs.

MYTH: The European Court of Human Rights will force religious organisations to conduct same-sex marriages.

REALITY: The case law of the European Court of Human Rights makes it clear that same-sex marriage is a matter for individual states to decide. Any case before the Court would be brought against the UK Government, not a religious organisation. The Court would be bound to give priority to the rights of a religious organisation under Article 9 of the European Convention on Human Rights, which guarantees the right to freedom of religion.

MYTH: The Church of England and Church in Wales have been banned by the Government from conducting same-sex marriages.

REALITY: This is not true. Like every other religious organisation, the Church of England and Church in Wales will be able to decide for themselves whether and when to allow the marrying of same-sex couples according to their rites. The Bill contains specific measures to deal with the unique legal position of the Church of England and the Church in Wales. Unlike any other religious body in this country, their clergy have a specific (common law) legal duty to marry parishioners. The Bill makes clear that this duty is not extended to marriage of same-sex couples, and will ensure that Anglican Canon law does not conflict with civil law and can continue to state that for them marriage is between one man and one woman.

MYTH: The Church of England and Church in Wales are being given extra protections.

REALITY: The Bill contains specific measures to deal with the unique legal position of the Church of England and the Church in Wales. The clergy of the Church of England and Church in Wales have a legal duty to marry parishioners. The Bill provides them with protection to address this point. The Bill also ensures that Church of England Canon law, which states their belief that marriage is between one man and one woman, is not affected by this Bill. These provisions are required

to take account of these Churches' particular legal circumstances – they do not provide more, or less, protection than is given to other religious organisations.

MYTH: The Church of England and Church in Wales were not consulted properly.

REALITY: During the course of both the consultation and the drafting of the legislation, the Government has had numerous and detailed discussions with stakeholders about the provisions within the Bill. These discussions have included a number of religious organisations including the Church of England, the Catholic Church and the Church in Wales.

MYTH: Teachers will have to promote same-sex marriage to pupils in sex and relationships education.

REALITY: This is not true. No teacher will be required to promote or endorse views which go against their beliefs. As with any other area of the curriculum teachers will of course be required to teach the factual position, that under the law marriage can be between opposite-sex couples and same-sex couples. There are many areas within teaching, particularly within faith schools, where this type of issue already arises and where subjects such as divorce are taught with sensitivity. The guidance governing these issues is the same guidance that will govern how same-sex marriage in the classroom will be approached. Sex and relationships education is categorically not about the promotion of a particular sexual orientation – that would be inappropriate teaching.

MYTH: Teachers who oppose same-sex marriage will be sacked from their jobs.

REALITY: Teachers will continue to have the clear right to express their own beliefs, or that of their faith in a professional way, such as that marriage should only be between a man and a woman. No teacher will be required to promote or endorse views which go against their beliefs.

MYTH: There is no difference between civil partnership and marriage.

REALITY: There are some small legal differences between civil partnerships and marriage. But for many people there are important differences in the perception of and responsibilities associated with these separate institutions.

MYTH: You are abolishing the terms 'husband', 'wife', 'mother' and 'father'.

REALITY: This is not true – these terms will continue to exist. 'Husband' will refer to a male marriage partner and 'wife' will refer to a female marriage partner, as now.

MYTH: Not introducing civil partnerships for opposite-sex couples is unfair.

REALITY: This is not true. We believe in the institution of marriage and we do not believe that opposite-sex couples are disadvantaged by not being able to enter into civil partnerships. This Bill is designed to remove the unfairness of same-sex couples being excluded from marriage.

MYTH: This is the thin end of the wedge – further changes to the law to enable other groups to marry are likely.

REALITY: This is simply not the case – we have absolutely no plans to amend the law on marriage in any other area.

MYTH: You did not take into account the large number of petitions received opposing a change in the law.

REALITY: 228,000 individuals and organisations responded to the consultation on how to open up marriage to same-sex couples. Additionally there were petitions for and against equal marriage. The largest was from the Coalition for Marriage against the proposals which contained over 500,000 signatures opposed to the proposals. The views expressed in the petitions were considered along with all the other responses received. However, the Government have always been clear that the consultation was focussed on *how* to implement a change in the law, rather than *whether* to change the law.

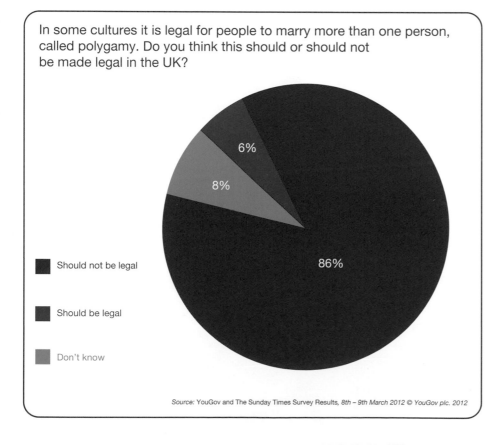

In some cultures it is legal for people to marry more than one person, called polygamy. Do you think this should or should not be made legal in the UK?

6%

8%

86%

■ Should not be legal

■ Should be legal

■ Don't know

Source: YouGov and The Sunday Times Survey Results, *8th – 9th March 2012 © YouGov plc. 2012*

MYTH: The Government has no mandate to introduce same-sex marriage.

REALITY: The Conservative Party's *A Contract for Equalities*, published alongside its General Election Manifesto in 2010, set out clearly that we would consider the case for changing the law to allow civil partnerships to be called and classified as marriage. Independent surveys, such as the one carried out by *The Times* in March 2012, show support by the general public with 65% thinking gay couples should have an equal right to marry, not just to have civil partnerships.

MYTH: People will be sacked if they criticise same-sex marriage at work.

REALITY: This is not true. We have always been absolutely clear that being able to follow your faith openly is a vital freedom that we will protect. Everyone is entitled to express their view about same-sex marriage, at work or elsewhere. No employee will be required to promote or endorse views about same-sex marriage which go against their conscience. But it is an entirely different matter to act in an offensive or discriminatory way because of someone's sexual orientation and the two issues should not be confused.

MYTH: The four recent European Court cases show that people are not free to follow their beliefs at work.

REALITY: On the contrary, Ms Eweida won her right to wear a cross at work. These cases were not about same-sex marriage. However, we have always been absolutely clear that being able to follow your faith openly is a vital freedom that we will protect. We believe people should be able to wear discrete religious symbols, provided it doesn't hinder or physically get in the way of their job. In the other cases the Court found that the needs of health and safety and the requirement not to discriminate against customers were relevant considerations, on

the facts of those particular cases – it is all about striking a sensible balance, which our legislation does.

MYTH: The Trafford Housing case with Adrian Smith shows that people can be sacked because of their religious beliefs.

REALITY: Adrian Smith actually won his case in the High Court, a judgment which shows that expressing views about this type of issue in a measured and non-offensive manner does not permit an employer to discipline an employee. Any such action by an employer would be unlawful.

MYTH: Local councils will stop giving religious groups contracts or letting them use their facilities if they refuse to conduct same-sex marriages.

REALITY: This is not true. The Equality Act 2010 protects people from being discriminated against because of religious belief. Treating someone in this way because of their religious opposition to same-sex marriage would be unlawful discrimination. It would also be a misuse of the council's powers if it penalised a religious body for doing something which is lawful.

MYTH: This Bill is being rushed through Parliament and has not been properly thought through.

REALITY: This is untrue. The Government is committed to introducing same-sex marriage and published a consultation in March 2012 which resulted in the biggest ever response to a UK consultation. The Minister for Women and Equalities made a statement to the house in December 2012 announcing the Government's intention to bring forward legislation.

MYTH: Polling shows that the public is not supportive of this policy.

REALITY: This is untrue. Recent polling shows that there are a range of views on this subject. We know that there are many people who are in favour of and supportive of this policy, as shown by 53% of people who responded to our consultation.

⇨ The above information is reprinted with kind permission from the Government Equalities Office. Please visit www.gov.uk for further information.

Marriage for all: it's time for civil partnerships to go

MPs are to vote on whether to allow straight couples to enter civil partnerships. However, Alice Arnold, currently in a civil partnership with Clare Balding, wants to see the end of them and instead, for marriage to be open to all.

By Alice Arnold

If you had asked me ten years ago whether I would like to get married my answer would have been an unequivocal 'no'. Then, when I was very happily in a relationship, and had been for four years, the perfect solution of civil partnership was offered to us.

I didn't like the idea of 'marriage'. The word itself had connotations of a patriarchal society. Maybe it still does. The defence that Vicky Pryce used of 'marital coercion' is still one that can only be used by a woman. The expectation that men are dominant in marriage is therefore enshrined in our law. But is this anachronistic?

MPs have tabled new amendments to the equal marriage legislation, that is currently going through Parliament, to give straight couples the same rights as homosexual ones, i.e. that straight couples should be able to choose to marry or enter into a civil partnership instead.

I gave evidence to the Parliament committee discussing equal marriage. I was teamed up for the session with the Very Reverend Jeffrey John, Dean of St Albans. Now I have always made it quite clear that I am not a religious person. In my life, marriage is a civil act that has nothing to do with the church. But Jeffrey is a wise man (he is also very entertaining and great company by the way) so I listened to what he had to say on this matter with great care.

He was against the rights of straight people to have civil partnerships for the reason that it would create a two-tier system. A sort of 'marriage light'. What would be the difference between marriage and civil partnerships? The legal rights are almost entirely the same. The difference for me has been in the word itself.

It is because of the word that I supported equal marriage. I was fed up with people asking me if I was married or not and having to reply that I wasn't BUT I was in a civil partnership... a sort of second best.

Maybe some people don't see it as second best? Maybe some people feel so strongly about the patriarchal associations of the word marriage that they want nothing to do with it? However, they do want the same legal rights that marriage would give them.

The connotations of a word can change. We can claim words for ourselves. My answer to this dilemma is not to have two legal systems to cement partnership but to claim 'marriage' for all of us. I want equality. I want to be able to have the same word to describe my relationship as straight people. I know that that word is recognised in all circles and in all nations.

What does a civil partnership mean? It means a lifetime commitment to another person. If there were to be a choice between marriage and civil partnerships for straight couples why would you choose to have a civil partnership? You would only choose it if the word marriage had bad connotations for you. Personally I think that any straight couple who made that choice would soon find out, as I did, that having to explain that you are not married but are in a civil partnership, is a clumsy and tedious exercise.

We are now in the awkward position. There are thousands of gay couples in civil partnerships. We will be given the right to 'upgrade' to marriage should we wish to. There will be some couples who do not wish to do this and they must have that right. You can't retrospectively change the agreement they entered into.

I hear straight people who are up in arms because gay couples will have the right to something extra and yes it's true we do. We have quite a lot of things straight couples don't have. We have centuries of discrimination, church leaders teaching that our very existence is an abomination and we have violent and threatening abuse. Would you like some of that too? No I didn't think so.

When gay couples can get married, that in itself will help to counteract the association of the word with patriarchal inequality. In my ideal world civil partnerships will naturally fizzle out. We will have one word. That word will be 'marriage' and we will all be proud of what it means.

14 March 2013

⇨ The above information is reprinted with kind permission from the Telegraph Media Group. Please visit www.telegraph.co.uk for further information.

© Alice Arnold/
The Daily Telegraph

But why would anyone want to get married?

Letters from The Independent readers.

I am bewildered by this ongoing discussion of whether and where gay people should be married – surely the real question is whether it's right for anyone to marry anyone, anywhere.

I believe that gay people should have the same rights as heterosexuals. I also believe that I have no right to dictate to others about their way of life. But I am saddened that so many apparently decent people still subscribe to the view that marriage is in any way respectable.

You can have the good things, the love, caring and commitment, without subscribing to the institution. And you can have the necessary things, the legal and financial stuff, in a civil partnership. Nothing is added by marriage, except the expectation of possession.

The notion that one person can have rights of ownership over another is not only ethically highly questionable but also pragmatically unsound. It has been shown that many species form lifelong pair bonds, but that individuals have the occasional 'fling' which does not necessarily threaten the primary relationship.

Humans, however, when their expectations are disappointed, often become vindictive and destructive, and families break apart.

Marriage was expedient, up to a point, when women were chattels. But life has moved on. Is it not time to acknowledge that outright ownership of your life's partner no longer works to support families?

I don't suggest casual sexual encounters should be encouraged, but it is undeniable that extramarital relationships happen. If you love someone, surely you must be willing occasionally to share them or let them go. And they are more likely to stay or come back if they are not subjected to personal and societal outrage.

Susan Alexander

Frampton Cotterell, Gloucestershire

30 December 2012

⇨ The above information is reprinted with kind permission from *The Independent*. Please visit www.independent.co.uk for further information.

The Rev Bernard O'Connor (letters, 28 December) suggests the word 'children' prevents gay marriage from being 'the same as marriage as we have always known it'.

There is no such thing as 'marriage as we have always known it'; its meaning has evolved. And marriage is not about creating children. If he believes otherwise, he should start asking couples to have fertility tests before he marries them.

David French

Edinburgh

I have yet to discover any difference, in practice, between civil partnership and marriage in a register office (probably the most usual sort of marriage now). Your leader (26 December) states that gay marriage would give gay couples 'full equality before the law'. If so, surely it would be simpler to review legislation on civil partnerships than to alter the dictionary definition of marriage.

If we do redefine the word marriage, will we also redefine words such as wife, husband, adultery and so on? Will quotes from literature have to be spelled out?

Will marriage mean any committed relationship? Presumably not or we may find ourselves 'married' to our dogs and cats. I expect it means any committed sexual relationship, but what sort of sex? Was President Clinton acting as if married to Monica Lewinsky or did he really 'not have sexual relations with that woman'?

Most importantly of all is equality; if we can't work towards a world in which people are different and equal, then we are in a mess.

Evelyn Adey

Athelington, Suffolk

Gay people divided over same-sex marriage

Catholic Voices survey of LGBT people.

The first ever professionally-conducted poll of gay people's attitudes to same-sex marriage has revealed widespread indifference to the Government's proposal. Only 39% think redefining marriage is a priority for gay people, only half say it is important to them personally, while just over one in four (27%) say they would get married if the law permitted it.

The poll reveals deep suspicion among gay people about David Cameron's motives (fewer than one in five believe the Prime Minister is backing the move out of conviction) while fewer than half accept Stonewall's argument that a legal distinction between civil partnerships and same-sex marriage perpetuates discrimination.

The online poll by ComRes for Catholic Voices surveyed 541 adults between 17 April and 20 May who describe themselves as gay/lesbian or bisexual. This is the first detailed study of gay peoples' attitudes to the Government's plans to redefine marriage. Among its most significant findings:

⇨ More than a quarter (26%) believe there is no need to change the law on marriage because civil partnerships give the same rights, while fewer than half agree with Stonewall's view that not allowing same-sex marriage worsens public attitudes to gay people.

⇨ Almost half believe 'David Cameron is only trying to extend marriage to LGBT people to make his party look more compassionate rather than because of his convictions', while only 19% disagree.

⇨ More than two-thirds (77%) of gay people disagree that marriage should be only between a man and a woman, and the same number (72%) believe 'marriage is more about love between two people than it is about rearing children'.

⇨ But only half (50%) of the LGBT population think it is important to extend marriage to same-sex couples, while just over one in four (27%) would marry their partner if the law allowed it – just one percentage point more than those not in a civil partnership who would seriously consider one.

ComRes first asked respondents to self-identify according to sexual orientation, before going on to ask the 5% who self-described as gay, lesbian, bisexual or other a series of questions about marriage as an institution, same-sex marriage and civil partnerships. The percentage of people self-identifying as gay was higher than the 2010 ONS Integrated Household Survey (which recorded 1.5% of the UK's population, or 726,000 people, as gay). The higher proportion in the ComRes poll may reflect that fact that online polls tend to attract younger, urban populations where numbers of openly gay people are higher.

ComRes surveyed a representative sample of 541 adults from 27 April to 20 May 2012 who self-identified as gay, lesbian, bisexual or other non-heterosexual. Data were weighted to be representative demographically of the wider GB adult population. ComRes is a member of the British Polling Council and abides by its rules.

27 April–20 May 2012

⇨ The above information is reprinted with kind permission from ComRes. Please visit www.comres.co.uk for further information.

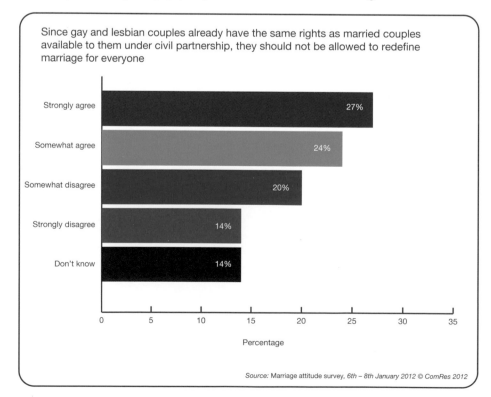

Since gay and lesbian couples already have the same rights as married couples available to them under civil partnership, they should not be allowed to redefine marriage for everyone

- Strongly agree: 27%
- Somewhat agree: 24%
- Somewhat disagree: 20%
- Strongly disagree: 14%
- Don't know: 14%

Percentage

Source: Marriage attitude survey, 6th – 8th January 2012 © ComRes 2012

© ComRes 2013

Religious Britons support gay marriage

YouGov poll for Stonewall shows three in five people of faith in Britain support same-sex marriage.

⇨ Extensive poll creates 'holes below waterline' for Bishop's objection to equal marriage

⇨ 83% say 'no problem' with a gay heir to the throne

A poll of more than 2,000 people conducted by YouGov for Stonewall has revealed that three in five people of faith support Government plans to extend civil marriage to same-sex couples, despite a vitriolic campaign against the proposal by some faith leaders.

Stonewall's five-yearly polling of public attitudes, for its 2012 *Living Together* report, shows that more than 80% of British adults under 50 now support the proposal.

The YouGov poll shows three in five people say there's still public prejudice against Britain's 3.7 million lesbian, gay and bisexual people, and four in five believe it's right to tackle that prejudice where they say it exists. The report also finds that more than four in five people would have no objection if the first child – and heir to the throne – of the Duke and Duchess of Cambridge grew up to be lesbian, gay or bisexual.

Stonewall Chief Executive Ben Summerskill said: 'Recently we've heard senior clerics distressingly compare marriage for gay people to polygamy, bestiality and child abuse. This polling holes below the waterline the suggestion that they speak for the majority of Britain's faith communities and vindicates years of campaigning by Stonewall to change public attitudes.'

Living Together 2012 also reveals, however, that in the last five years, 2.4 million people of working age have witnessed verbal homophobic bullying at work and 800,000 people of working age have witnessed physical homophobic bullying at work. Two thirds of people aged 18

to 29 say there was homophobic bullying in their school.

'Although the research contains good news,' said Ben Summerskill, 'it's also clear there's a lot of work to be done before 21st-century Britain is truly tolerant. We'll not rest until every single lesbian, gay or bisexual young person grows up in a country where they're afforded exactly the same dignity and respect as their heterosexual counterparts.'

Survey consisted of 2,074 adults from across England, Scotland and Wales. Fieldwork was undertaken online between 25 November and 5 December 2011. The figures have been weighted and are representative of adults across Britain.

13 June 2012

⇨ The above information is reprinted with kind permission from YouGov. Please visit www.yougov.co.uk for further information.

© 2000–2013 YouGov plc

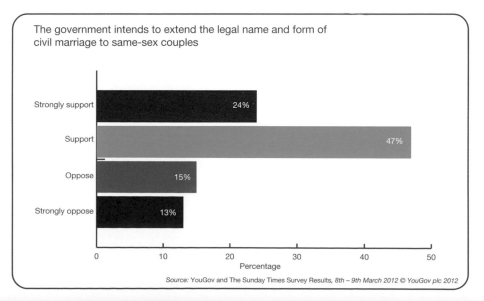

The government intends to extend the legal name and form of civil marriage to same-sex couples

	Percentage
Strongly support	24%
Support	47%
Oppose	15%
Strongly oppose	13%

Source: YouGov and The Sunday Times Survey Results, 8th – 9th March 2012 © YouGov plc 2012

Ending a marriage or civil partnership

Divorce

You can get a divorce if you have been married at least a year and your relationship has permanently broken down.

You must have a marriage that is legally recognised in the UK, and have a permanent home in England or Wales.

There are three main steps to getting divorced:

⇨ File a divorce petition – you have to apply to the court for permission to divorce, and show reasons why you want the marriage to end.

⇨ Apply for a decree nisi – if your spouse agrees to the petition, you'll get a document saying there's no reason you can't divorce.

⇨ Apply for a decree absolute – this legally ends your marriage – you need to wait six weeks after you get the decree nisi before you can apply.

Arrange your own divorce

You may be able to arrange your own divorce without involving solicitors if you agree on:

⇨ the reasons for a divorce

⇨ how you'll look after any children

⇨ how you'll split up money, property and possessions.

If you agree on these things beforehand, you won't have to go to a court hearing, and the divorce paperwork should be fairly straightforward.

Grounds for divorce

You must show there are good reasons for ending your marriage.

You can give five grounds for a divorce:

1. Adultery

Your husband or wife had sex with someone else of the opposite sex, and you can no longer bear to live with them.

You can't give adultery as a reason if you lived with your husband or wife for six months after you found out about it.

2. Unreasonable behaviour

Your husband or wife behaved so badly that you can no longer bear to live with them.

This could include:

⇨ physical violence

⇨ verbal abuse, e.g. insults or threats

⇨ drunkenness or drug-taking

⇨ refusing to pay for housekeeping.

3. Desertion

Your husband or wife has left you:

⇨ without your agreement

⇨ without a good reason

⇨ to end your relationship

⇨ for more than two years in the past two-and-a-half years.

You can still claim desertion if you have lived together for up to a total of six months in this period.

4. You have lived apart for more than two years

You can get a divorce if you've lived apart for more than two years and both agree to the divorce.

Your husband or wife must agree in writing.

5. You have lived apart for more than five years

Living apart for more than five years is usually enough to get a divorce, even if your husband or wife disagrees with the divorce.

Ending a civil partnership

You can apply to end ('dissolve') your civil partnership if you have been in the partnership for at least a year.

There are three main steps to ending a civil partnership:

⇨ File a dissolution petition – you have to apply to court for permission to end your civil partnership, and show reasons why you want to split up.

⇨ Apply for a conditional order – if your civil partner agrees to the petition, you'll get a document saying there's no reason you can't divorce.

⇨ Apply for a final order – this legally ends your civil partnership – you need to wait six weeks after you get the conditional order before you can apply.

Ending a civil partnership without using solicitors

You may be able to arrange your own divorce without involving solicitors if you agree on:

⇨ the reasons for dissolving the civil partnership

⇨ how you'll split up money, property and possessions

⇨ how you'll look after any children.

If you agree on these things beforehand, you won't have to go to a court hearing, and the paperwork should be fairly straightforward.

Grounds for ending a civil partnership

You have to show the relationship has irretrievably broken down, and that you have good reasons for ending the civil partnership.

There are four grounds for ending a civil partnership:

1. Unreasonable behaviour

Your partner has behaved so badly that you can no longer bear to live with them.

This could include:

⇨ physical or mental cruelty

⇨ verbal or physical abuse

⇨ being irresponsible with money

⇨ being sexually unfaithful.

2. Desertion

Your partner has left you:

⇨ without your agreement

⇨ without a good reason

⇨ to end your relationship

⇨ for more than two years in the past two-and-a-half years.

You can still claim desertion if you have lived together for up to a total of six months within this period.

3. You have lived apart for more than two years

You can get a dissolution if you have lived apart for more than two years, and both agree to end the civil partnership.

Your civil partner must agree in writing to end the civil partnership.

4. You have lived apart for more than five years

Living apart for more than five years is usually enough to end a civil partnership, even if your civil partner disagrees.

⇨ The above information is reprinted with kind permission from gov. uk. Please visit www.gov.uk for further information.

Startling new research on UK divorce rate

Divorce rate unchanged since the 1960s after ten years of marriage, says new research.

A new report from The Marriage Foundation think-tank, *What is the divorce rate?*, has shattered the common assumption that the divorce rate for all couples is higher than it was in the 1960s.

Looking at the rate of divorce over the last four decades, Harry Benson, Communications Director at The Marriage Foundation, found that the divorce rate for couples after they have been married for ten years or more was the same as it was in the 1970s, 80s, 90s and 2000s.

A couple who married in 2001 have the same chance of getting divorced after ten or more years of marriage as a couple who married in 1971, a consistency Mr Benson describes as 'remarkable'.

One in five newlyweds divorce after ten years of marriage, with the likelihood of a marriage ending in divorce further shrinking with each decade. A tiny two per cent of weddings end in divorce after 30 years of marriage, with divorce rates after 40 years of marriage even rarer: fewer than 0.5 per cent of couples divorce after being married 40 years or more.

Details of the new research will be presented by Mr Benson at the launch of National Marriage Week at 6pm in the Macmillan Room at the House of Commons on Thursday 7 February.

Mr Benson says: 'All the change in divorce rates since the 1960s have occurred during the first ten years of marriage. After ten years of marriage, there's the same chance a couple who marry in 2013 will keep the vow 'death do us part' as there was 40 years ago.'

Half of all divorces currently take place during the first decade of marriage. There is hope for newlyweds, however, in that the divorce rate during the first ten years of marriage has fallen in recent years from a peak in 1993, a trend Mr Benson predicts will continue.

He adds: 'Changes in divorce rates during the first ten years reflect the care we take in forming our relationship in the first place. Couples who marry today are clearly making better choices, with fewer marriages breaking down in the very early years than in the 1990s and early 2000s.'

Within the first decade of marriage, the highest number of divorces occurs between three and six years of marriage, debunking the myth of the 'seven year itch'. After peaking between three and six years, the likelihood of a marriage ending in divorce decreases with each year thereafter.

Mr Benson concluded: 'A couple who tie the knot on Valentine's Day this year have a 39 per cent chance of divorcing during their lifetime.

'The so-called silver surfers – couples divorcing in their twilight years after many decades of marriage – is greatly overhyped and not supported by statistical evidence.

'Our research reveals that if a married couple survive the first ten years of marriage, their risk of divorce is the same as it has been in the previous four decades.'

6 February 2013

⇨ Information from The Marriage Foundation. Please visit www. marriagefoundation.org.uk for further information.

Teens and divorce: the kids are not all right

As Chris Huhne now knows only too well, divorce can hurt teens just as much as children – if not more.

Ten years ago, if anyone had told me they were postponing divorce 'till the children are older' I'd have thought their words made perfect sense. Back then, my children were one, five, eight and 10. I wouldn't have been able to imagine the effect on them of hearing that their father and I were splitting up. Whose house would they live in? How would they cope without bedtime cuddles from both of us? What would weekends and holidays be like for them without the two of us around? So much better to postpone it, I'd have mused: by the time they were older and living their own lives, they'd hardly even notice the break-up.

Today, though, my elder daughters are almost 21 and 18 – and I now realise that, however hard it would have been for them to cope with a family split when they were younger, it would, if anything, be worse for them to have to face it now. And if I already knew that somewhere deep inside the fallout on the son of Chris Huhne and Vicky Pryce from their break-up, as tragically documented during last week's court case, only underlines the issues.

Peter Huhne was 18 when his parents' marriage ended. To the outside world he'd have looked, just as my daughters look, like adults. But inside he was sometimes still a child – just as my daughters are still sometimes children – and when things went sour between the two people who mattered most in the world to him, he found it very hard to handle. His passionate, angry text messages to his father, made public after Chris Huhne's guilty plea, lay bare his confusion and hurt and horror that the break-up could be happening – not only to them, but to him.

> **"Divorce doesn't just happen to a couple, it also happens (if they have them) to their children"**

And that, really, is the point: divorce doesn't just happen to a couple, it also happens (if they have them) to their children. And it happens to those children whether they are babies or small children or big children or even adult children: because for most of us, our parents' marriage is the bedrock on which our lives are built. It's a vital part of our stability at any age: when I was in my 40s, the fact that my parents were still together (my father has since died) and the fact that they had a home together that I could visit and to which I could take my children gave a layer of certainty, of permanence, even at that stage of my life.

But if your parents' divorce is going to hit you at any age, it's probably going to hit you especially badly when you're a young adult.

'People make the assumption that because someone is legally an adult, they are emotionally an adult – but that's not true,' says the Cambridge University psychologist Terri

QUICK-CALL A SOCIOLOGIST!!

Apter, who has written extensively on the transition from adolescence to adulthood. 'In fact, the brain doesn't become fully adult until the age of about 24. Until that stage, you're dealing with people who don't have the psychological hardiness of an adult: they can't properly plan ahead or master their impulses the way an adult can.'

Being grown-up is often equated with leaving home – but, Apter says, this is a misunderstanding. 'They may have physically left home for part of the year to study, but it's vitally important for them to be closely connected with their family and the home they grew up in. Of course they want to be independent, and they're practising independence, but being able to do that relies to a very large extent on knowing that their parents and their home are behind them.'

"If you've got children, ending a marriage is never going to be straightforward"

So in other words, the existence of a dull, boring, samey old home being somewhere in the background gives young adults the confidence to strike out and try living in a different sort of way. But if that home and that family crumble, the story is very different: young people start to question everything they've come to know as true and strong and feeling the rug pulled from under them can lead them to question all sorts of assumptions in their lives. Suddenly, everything they thought was real isn't real. They start to wonder whether their parents ever loved one another, whether their marriage has been a total sham. They may feel guilt: did their parents stay together this long just because of them? And if so, what unhappiness has their existence heaped on them? Beyond that, Apter says, there's a kind of emotional displacement. Young adults don't need their parents in the way they did when they were children – but they still need lots

of psychological support. They fall in and out of love, they have work crises, they struggle with what they're going to do with their lives, they fret about how they're going to afford a flat. All these problems need a lot of time and a lot of energy from their parents. And if those parents are caught up in their own problems and are negotiating the end of a long marriage, there won't be much emotional energy left to help their children.

Right through our lives, there's a sense in all of us that we have to be the 'stars' where our parents are concerned. And divorcing parents, especially those going through messy divorces like the Huhnes's, take centre-stage and edge their children into the wings, every single time.

There's no doubt either that the ending of their parents' marriage has implications for the relationships their young adult children are embarking on. Research by the Joseph Rowntree Foundation found that people who were over 20 when their parents separated were more likely to have their own first partnership or marriage break up by the age of 33. And there are financial implications, too: when parents stay together, the family pot stays

intact. Separated, their individual needs eat more quickly into their savings and there will be fewer funds to support children as they set out on their own lives and less for them when their parents eventually die.

It's all sobering stuff, especially given that the number of so-called 'silver splitters' (couples whose marriages break up in their late 40s and 50s) is on the rise.

The bottom line is, if you've got children, ending a marriage is never going to be straightforward. But the important thing, Apter says, is knowing that's the case. 'Everyone understands how much support young children need if their parents split up,' she says. 'But they need just as much support and help when they're adults as well – and providing that support makes a huge difference as to how their lives pan out.'

12 February 2013

⇨ The above information is reprinted with kind permission from The Independent. Please visit www.independent.co.uk for further information.

© *independent.co.uk 2013*

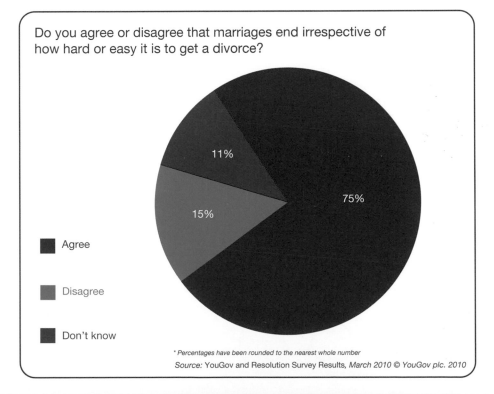

Do you agree or disagree that marriages end irrespective of how hard or easy it is to get a divorce?

11%
15%
75%

- Agree
- Disagree
- Don't know

Percentages have been rounded to the nearest whole number
Source: YouGov and Resolution Survey Results, *March 2010* © *YouGov plc. 2010*

Government launches divorce app

Help for separating parents at their fingertips as new web app launches. A third of children now live in separated families.

For the first time, the 300,000 families undergoing separation every year in Britain will be able to get free online advice tailored to their needs.

The Government is today (Thursday) launching an easy-to-use web app, called 'Sorting out Separation', featuring an innovative and interactive tool, which offers parents personalised advice and shows where they can access further support.

Around five million parents have gone through separation and the new figures show over four million children now live in separated families – equal to a third of children in Britain.

However, a YouGov poll out today commissioned by the DWP reveals that more than half of parents (52%) find it hard to access help and support they need when they separate.

Work and Pensions Minister, Steve Webb, said:

'Parents tell us they don't know where to turn for support when they're going through a separation. A third of British children now live in separated families and it's vital we help parents to access better advice. Parents working together is in the best interests of the children, and more collaboration helps minimise the impact of separation on them.

'That's why we're launching a new web app, named Sorting out Separation and hosted by leading parenting websites, to give people support tailored to their needs.'

Sorting out Separation is a one-stop-shop for any parent going through a separation. It covers everything from how to avoid a separation to coping with the emotional impact of breaking up, accessing legal or housing support and arranging child maintenance. The web app will be hosted by a range of leading family websites, starting with the likes of Relate, National Family Mediation, Mumsnet, Dad.info, Gransnet and Wikivorce.

Other findings from the new YouGov survey show:

⇨ 39% of parents didn't access any professional support when they separated from their partners, of whom 25% said it was because they couldn't find the right help or support or felt embarrassed.

⇨ Of those parents who did seek professional help, 27% of them felt they received conflicting advice.

The Department for Work and Pensions worked closely with the Department for Education and Ministry of Justice in developing the new service, in conjunction with the voluntary and community sector. It forms part of a £20 million fund announced earlier this year to help support separating parents.

Ruth Sutherland, CEO of Relate, commented:

'We know more than anyone the profound difficulties that relationship breakdown can throw up for people. Finding the support to overcome these issues can be challenging, so the Government should be commended for introducing this new web app. We're pleased that it will help people identify the help they need and direct them to support – and we're proud to be hosting it.'

Justine Roberts, CEO and co-founder of Mumsnet, said:

'The beauty of this new service is that parents thinking of separating won't need to go to great lengths to seek it out. We're pleased the Government is using technology cleverly to bring resources to the people who need it.'

Ken Sanderson, CEO of Families Need Fathers, also welcomed the app:

'We're very happy to be involved in this initiative. We're confident it will help separating families more easily access the wealth of specialist support services out there to help them reach arrangements focused on what's best for their children.'

29 November 2012

⇨ The above information is reprinted with kind permission from the Department for Work & Pensions. Please visit www.dwp.gov.uk for further information.

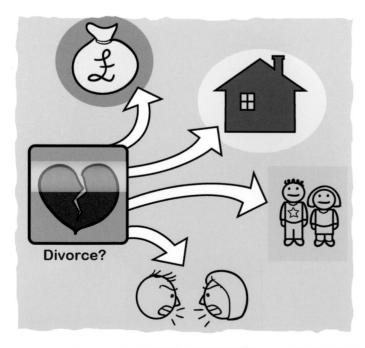

Divorce?

DIY divorce comes with a health warning

From the Mills & Reeve divorce law blog.

By Rachel Chapman

The national press is littered with articles about the steep costs of divorce and horror stories of people who have spent tens of thousands of pounds (or even more – remember the divorcing solicitors who started with millions and ended up with £90,000?) for a service that they probably never envisaged they would need. This, combined with the ongoing economic uncertainty we face and the fact that legal aid for most divorcing couples is about to be pulled, is reason enough to seek a 'cheaper' alternative to instructing solicitors. As a result, there is a growing trend for so-called DIY divorces, where you deal with the divorce process by using an online service.

Many people understandably want what is one of the most distressing times in their lives over with as quickly and cheaply as possible. However, appearances can be deceptive. Websites offering 'quickie' divorces can come with a price if you're not careful.

"There is a growing trend for so-called DIY divorces, where you deal with the divorce process by using an online service"

It's true to say that the divorce process is paper-based and, more often than not, you do not need to attend court to get to decree absolute (the final decree that ends the marriage). But there are many issues that can't be sorted out by a simple online form. What if your spouse contests the divorce or does not agree costs? What if you need to hold up the divorce to protect your position if your spouse dies before you've finalised the money aspects? These require proper advice and even court hearings that cannot be dealt with over the Internet.

More importantly, the relatively straightforward administrative process of the divorce itself is not the end of the story of course. The key issues of the arrangements for your children and your finances need to be dealt with.

Issues relating to the children can be the most emotional for both parents. Where the children are going to live, where they will spend Christmas and where they will go to school are all things that will need to be discussed by the family, but are often the most contentious. Although only a minority of families end up in court, specialist advice early on makes it more likely that you will be able to agree on what's best for your children. You can't pay a quick one-off fee to cover this.

It's vital of course that you understand and try to reach agreement on the financial consequences of your divorce. What assets you have as a family and how they should be split fairly are key issues. Professional advice is needed to make sure that everything is considered and covered. Your future financial security depends on it.

There is a common misconception that the party at fault, for example the person who had an affair, is 'punished' financially. This is simply not the case. If you can't agree and the court ends up having to decide it will take a number of factors into consideration. What you may think is fair and appropriate may not be, for example if you simply hadn't appreciated the importance of pensions or the value of some business interests.

There is no question that in the short run completing the divorce process online can be cheaper, but what about the long-term costs? If there are issues left unresolved between you and your spouse, how can you be sure that you will obtain a fair and complete settlement?

"At one of the most important and emotional periods of your life you can't afford to get it wrong"

Involving professionals will provide protection for you and your family in the future by ensuring that you have not missed any details or failed to close any loopholes. The law surrounding divorce and finances is so fluid that you need someone who is experienced and up to date.

Lawyers are not the only professionals who can help you. Mediation or collaborative law may be good options for you to consider. A settlement that you both agree on after checking that you have all the relevant information is almost always going to be better than one imposed on you by a judge at the end of lengthy and costly court proceedings.

DIY has its place, but at one of the most important and emotional periods of your life you can't afford to get it wrong.

29 January 2013

⇨ The above information is reprinted with kind permission from divorce.co.uk. Please visit www.divorce.co.uk for further information.

© divorce.co.uk 2013

Children affected by separation

Evidence shows that the effects of separation on children can be limited.

It is estimated that one in three children in the UK will experience parental separation before the age of 16. Approximately half of couples divorcing in 2010 had at least one child aged under 16, and over a fifth were under age five.

The number of children affected by divorce has risen over the past few decades, from about 82,000 (under 16 years) in 1971 to 100,000 in 2009.

It is difficult to say exactly how many cohabiting couples with children separate, but the number is likely to be substantial. As many as 30% of all births in England and Wales in 2008 were to unmarried parents living at the same address, many of whom will have been cohabiting. Cohabiting couples are more likely to split up, and one in three cohabiting parents separate before their child's fifth birthday, compared to about one in ten who are married.

Considering these facts, the total number of children who are affected by the separation of their biological parents is likely to be much greater than the number affected by divorce alone.

The impact of relationship breakdown on children is just one area investigated in When couples part: *Understanding the consequences for adults and children*. This in-depth review considers the evidence for the many and varied issues associated with relationship stress and breakdown. The report also provides guidance on what might be done to alleviate these problems.

Short- and long-term effects of break up on children

Most commonly, children of separated couples will experience greater poverty.

Studies have also shown that children whose biological parents have split up have worse outcomes in terms of social, emotional and cognitive development, on average. This association remains regardless of whether the parents were married or cohabiting when the child was born.

A child's psychological and physical health can suffer. Children of separated parents are also more likely to have behavioural problems, exhibit anti-social behaviour and to take part in substance misuse.

Children of separated couples also tend to perform worse at school and have poorer future employment prospects. Research also shows that children of separated couples are less likely to have successful relationships themselves as adults.

Do all children of separated couples have problems?

No. It is not inevitable that all children will suffer long-term harm from the break up of a relationship. In fact, if there are good relations between the parents, most are able to adjust to the new family situation after an initial period of unhappiness and instability. The quality of parenting, a lack of financial hardship and whether or not the parents go through multiple relationships following the separation are also thought to be key to the wellbeing of the child.

Having parents that get along better together when they live apart is better for a child than being part of a dysfunctional family unit with high levels of destructive conflict. However, without such support many children do suffer negative consequences of a break up.

Who is affected the most by separation: boys or girls?

There is mixed opinion on whether boys or girls are affected most by the breakdown of a relationship. Although there is evidence showing that boys find separation more upsetting to begin with, there is also evidence that the effects on girls are more likely to last longer.

Studies also seem to show that boys find it easier to adjust to step families than girls, particularly if the girl is in early adolescence.

Older boys and girls tend to find it more difficult to adjust to step families than younger children. It has also been suggested, however, that younger children may not be aware of their parents' marital problems and so the separation itself may be a greater shock. This in turn can result in greater confusion and anxiety, and may lead to children blaming themselves for the separation.

The impact of new partners and families

There also appears to be an association between behaviour problems and the number of later relationships the parents have. These later relationships become transitional periods for the child, where they have to attune themselves to either living with a single parent, co-parenting or the introduction of their parents' new partners or step families.

The evidence shows that having multiple transitions can impact on behaviour problems such as disobedience and hyperactivity. Studies have shown that many children find the remarriage of a parent more stressful than the divorce.

Other research has shown that children may find it easier to deal with a parent's new partner if the other biological parent is not establishing a new relationship at the same time Having a stable family situation in at least one home seems to be important.

Limiting the effect of separation on children

The evidence indicates that the effects of separation on children can be limited, and the child can emerge free of any long-term harm. Although there is no comprehensive formula to follow to ensure a positive outcome for the child, a number of key factors seem to be associated with this:

⇨ Competent and warm parenting from both parents

⇨ Continuing good relations and co-operation between parents

⇨ Social support for the child such as extended family and friends.

Other factors that may increase the risk of poor outcomes include:

⇨ Maternal mental health

⇨ Financial hardship

⇨ A continued high level of conflict between parents

⇨ A lack of post-separation contact (where appropriate)

⇨ A lack of open communication between parent and child about the separation

⇨ Recurring changes in family circumstances.

⇨ The above information is reprinted with kind permission from OnePlusOne. Please visit www.oneplusone.org.uk for further information.

The benefits of being divorced

By Kimberly Seltzer, from The Art of Charm.

When you are divorced, it's easy to look at married couples and mourn the relationship you once had. There are often constant pressures from friends, family and society to be married. Marriage certainly can be a beautiful and wonderful thing, but so can divorce. It doesn't have to be all gloom and doom and filled with desperation. I propose that it can be, in fact, an exciting opportunity. Embrace your new life as a divorced man by using your freedom to meet new people and discover what you really want. I would even go so far to say that there are certain benefits to being divorced:

1. 'You' Time: If you have kids and have a joint custody agreement, you may actually have some time to yourself now that you're divorced. As a married man, your time was likely divided between your kids, work and spouse. You really had to make a conscious effort and get permission to have time for yourself. Now that you are single, there may be an opportunity to have some downtime and do things that you enjoy. It's OK to be selfish and indulge in activities that make you happy. What are things you liked to do when you were younger prior to the marriage? Do them!

2. 'You' Vacations: Gone are the days that you have to worry about where your partner wants to go. You can plan to go to a destination that you've always wanted to go to on your own. Use this as an opportunity to go places you haven't explored yet. Also, it's easier to meet new people on vacation; you tend to be more relaxed and people are naturally more open to meeting others when away from their home towns. So leave the computer at home, turn off your phone and hit the beach!

3. 'You' Activities and Festivities: It's exciting to pick and choose different activities and festivities that you enjoy. You don't have to attend parties that your spouse would like you to go to or talk to people that you are 'supposed' to talk to. Now you can concentrate on things that will be fun for you and engage in hobbies that you are passionate about – maybe even mingle with interesting women. Get a new outfit and hit some parties and networking events. You may meet some other single friends or a new woman with whom to do activities that you both appreciate.

4. 'You' Family Gatherings: Holidays and special occasions are often stressful while married because you have to figure out how to divide the time spent with each family, no matter what your relationship was like with your ex in-laws. Of course, after divorce there will be aspects that you will miss about the large family gatherings, but there are some perks to planning your own celebrations. Use this time to relax and be with your family. You might even start new traditions.

5. 'You' Makeover: Use this opportunity to really take care of your body and create a new image. Buy new clothes that make you feel amazing. Exercise and eat healthier. Often when you are married, you get stuck in a rut and you don't carve out time to take care of yourself. Exercise is a great way to re-focus your energy, get in shape and have that 'you' time. Also, you'll sleep better, feel invigorated and have the confidence to date again.

It's natural to feel the absence of the family unit and the partnership you once had. But the time after divorce is also a period where you can embrace your new freedom, create new celebrations, rejoice in the blessings you have and open yourself up to possibilities to come!

21 January 2013

⇨ The above article is reprinted with kind permission from the author, Kimberly Seltzer. Please visit theartofcharm.com/kimberly-seltzer for further information.

Trapped: the former couples who can't afford to move on

Stuck in the 'struggling middle', more ex-partners are unable to take on the burden of running two homes. And the problem is creeping up the income ladder, counsellors warn.

Middle-income couples, recently identified by the Conservatives as the 'struggling middle', are increasingly unable to afford to separate when their relationships end, according to a new study.

Almost half the counsellors surveyed at Relate, the charity that specialises in relationship counselling, say an increasing proportion of the 150,000 clients they see each year are being forced to remain living together despite having decided to split up. Couples with children are more likely to find themselves trapped than those without, but both groups are increasingly finding it impossible to bear the cost of setting up different homes.

'When we talk about Relate's clients, we are not talking about people on low incomes. We're talking about people in employment, on average to above-average incomes,' said Ruth Sutherland, the charity's chief executive.

Sutherland said the charity, which began life as the Marriage Guidance Council 75 years ago, had never seen this demographic of clients struggling with their finances to such an extent that moving into two homes and getting on with their lives was an impossibility.

'These are people who could previously afford to move away from each other when their relationship broke down,' she added. 'But now, they are stretched just to pay their mortgage on top of the rising cost of living. When their relationship breaks down, they find they can't afford two mortgages, on top of the cost of running two homes.'

Sutherland said that for parents, the cost of childcare was another devastating factor. Parents in the UK spend an average of 27% of their salary on childcare, compared with a European average of 13%. 25 hours of nursery care a week for a child aged two or under costs on average £5,000 in England, rising to between £6,000 and £15,000 in London.

'To pay for the increased childcare demands that come with being a single parent has become a pipe dream for many people, even those in well-paid jobs,' said Sutherland.

Richer couples could find themselves in the same predicament as the difficult economic climate continued, Sutherland predicted. 'I would not be surprised at all to see the problem creeping up the salary band,' she said. 'This era of austerity we're in is not like other hard times we have lived through.

'In the past, we've had a dip and then recovery, but now we're in unknown territory about the length of time people are going to have to cope with debt, job insecurity, pressure from work and the mounting cost of childcare.

'The only thing we know is that people are going to have to cope with these problems for longer than they would ever have done so before.'

At least 40% of Relate counsellors said they were seeing more couples split up than two years ago, with money worries cited as a major cause.

'It's vital for the future of our children, and thus the future health of our nation, that estranged parents manage their separation well,' said Sutherland.

'Children learn about relationships at home. If they see their parents undermining each other, arguing and being vindictive, then that's the foundation on which they will build their own relationships. It's not only the adults who, if stuck in a toxic situation, are going to be damaged.'

Which is why, said Sutherland, she was so concerned by another finding in Relate's survey: that separated couples are increasingly unable to afford to complete their counselling courses.

At least 80% of counsellors said increasing numbers of clients were unable to afford to 'properly start or conclude' their counselling programmes, despite being offered short, intensive courses of four to six sessions, charged from £6 to £45 an hour, depending on their income.

Over 70% of Relate counsellors said money problems including debt, a lack of disposable income, unemployment and rising living costs had worsened for their clients in the last two years.

Almost 90% of counsellors said money worries made their clients depressed, with 80% saying couples argued more as a result and 65% saying it affected their clients' physical health.

'Let's all be clear about the real cost of austerity: the impact of being in a relationship that isn't working is toxic. It is harmful to your children and it permeates every other aspect of your life,' said Sutherland. 'If the Government wanted to protect the mental health of the country, both now and in the future, they would target these cuts differently.'

The rate of family breakdown in the UK was revealed in October statistics from the Department of Work and Pensions showing that 79% of children under one live with both birth parents. This drops to 55% by the time the children reach 15.

Nearly a quarter of people have continued to live with a partner, or know someone who has, because they couldn't afford to live apart, according to a 2010 report from

Shelter. 'We also know that relationship breakup is a major cause of homelessness,' said Campbell Robb, chief executive of Shelter.

The 2012 total cost of family breakdown to the UK was £44 billion, up from £42 billion in 2011, according to a recent study by the Relationships Foundation. The study looked at the cost of family breakdown in five key areas of public policy: tax and benefits, housing, health and social care, civil and criminal justice, and education and young people not in education, employment or training (Neets). It concluded that the annual cost for each taxpayer was now £1,470.

'The Government's austerity policies are making things worse, and it doesn't make sense economically,' said Sutherland. 'What we want is for them to do a relationship and family impact assessment for every policy they consider introducing.'

Robb said the 'shortage of affordable housing in this country is being felt further and further up the income scale'.

'We're hearing from couples moving in together too fast to help with housing costs but then unable to move out if things go wrong because they can't afford to live on their own. This has a huge impact on people's home lives,' he added.

Robb said the housing crisis is 'the result of... more and more people chasing fewer and fewer homes, which has pushed up house prices and rents far faster than wages have risen.

'Our research also shows that more and more people are putting off having children because they can't find an affordable home,' he said. 'Something is badly wrong when people who are working hard still face a constant struggle to get a decent place to live.'

Caroline Davey, director of policy at Gingerbread, the charity for single-parent families, said families in the low- to middle-income bracket were 'increasingly struggling financially'. 'When a couple separates this financial squeeze can make it impossible for them to forge new lives separately,' she said.

'With wages stagnating, higher risk of redundancy, spiralling living costs, and many families without any savings to speak of, it can be simply unachievable for a separating couple to afford to run two homes rather than one. The only alternative for some families is to continue living in the same home but as separate households.'

Davey warned: 'This situation could become more commonplace in future as the financial downturn bites even harder on families across the income scale.'

She added: 'Action is needed across a number of areas, for example strengthening the role of local authorities in supporting access to private rented accommodation, reversing the harshest housing benefit cuts, and sustained job creation.'

A spokeswoman for the Treasury said: 'The Government has taken action to help people with the cost of living, including freezing council tax and fuel duty and cutting income tax for 25 million people by raising the personal allowance. Action taken to reduce the deficit has helped to keep interest rates near record lows. And we have extended the offer of 15 hours free education and care a week for disadvantaged two-year-olds, to cover an extra 130,000 children.'

20 November 2012

⇨ The above information is reprinted with kind permission from the Press Association. Please visit www.pressassociation.com.

© 2013 Press Association

Case study

Adela and Tanek married in Poland in 2002 and came to Britain with their two children four years later. For a few years, they lived comfortably: Adela worked full-time as an administrator, and Tanek in a factory. 'Our finances were fine – more than fine,' said Adela. 'We were living well and saving money. The children were happy and life was good.'

Two years ago, however, the couple broke up. Adela moved into a studio flat. The parents shared custody of the children but Tanek had returned to university and, soon afterwards, Adela's office closed down. Money became tight.

'Despite the problems, we would have had enough money but rents were going up and the cost of living rose sky high,' said Adela. 'We found that we just couldn't run two households, no matter how cheaply we lived. I didn't want to move into a single room because I wanted the children to live with me for half the week.

'It was a difficult decision and a terrible step backwards, but we eventually decided we had no choice but for me to move back into the family home.'

They are forced to share a bed but Adela said that, in one way, she and Tanek were fortunate. 'We get on well as friends but this situation is terribly awkward and very wrong. We want to get on with our lives and meet new people but we're stuck together.

'We can't afford a second bed and have nowhere to put one anyway. We don't have a sofa we can sleep on and we don't want the children to have to share their room with one of us.'

They hope that when Tanek finishes his degree next year, they will be able to afford to live separately. 'But who knows?' said Adela. 'The way the economic situation is at the moment, he might be unemployed for a long time.'

Key facts

- If you are 16 or 17 you cannot marry without parental consent. (page 1)

- The first recorded evidence of marriage contracts and ceremonies dates to 4,000 years ago, in Mesopotamia. In the ancient world, marriage served primarily as a means of preserving power, with kings and other members of the ruling class marrying off daughters to forge alliances, acquire land, and produce legitimate heirs. Even in the lower classes, women had little say over whom they married. (page 4)

- In 2005 the Home Office declared that forced marriages are a form of domestic violence and an abuse of human rights. (page 5)

- According to research from the Centre for Social Justice, marriage is being abandoned to the point where it's estimated that by 2031 only 57 per cent of families will be headed by a married couple, falling to just 49.5 per cent by 2047. (page 6)

- The average age for a woman's first marriage has climbed from 23.2 in 1981, when Prince Charles married 20-year-old Lady Diana Spencer, to 30 in 2011, when Prince William wed 29-year-old Catherine Middleton. (page 7)

- According to the Office of National Statistics, 3.7% more couples headed up the aisle in 2010 than had the previous year. (page 11)

- A third of marriages which take place in England and Wales don't last 15 years. (page 11)

- Of 1,735 contacts to the Forced Marriage Unit in 2010, 14 per cent involved a male victim and 86 per cent a female victim. (page 12)

- Over the last decade, 58 million young women – one in three – in developing countries have been married before the age of 18. The highest rates of marriage before 18 (generally considered to be child marriage) are found in Africa. In Niger, 75 per cent of girls marry before 18; in Chad, 72 per cent; and in Mali, 71 per cent. (page 15)

- The Civil Partnership Act came into force on 5 December 2005. By 31 March 2006 a total of 6,516 Civil Partnerships had been registered in England and Wales, 343 in Scotland and 43 in Northern Ireland. (page 18)

- MPs have voted by a majority of 225 in favour of the new Marriage (Same Sex Couples) Bill (passed by 400 to 175 votes). (page 20)

- YouGov polling for Stonewall shows that 71% of people in Britain support equal marriage. This figure rises to 82% of those under the age of 50. (page 20)

- Seven in ten people want to keep marriage as it is. (page 22)

- Over 3,000 laws make reference to marriage. (page 22)

- Only 39% think redefining marriage is a priority for gay people, only half say it is important to them personally, while just over one in four (27%) say they would get married if the law permitted it. (page 28)

- Stonewall's five-yearly polling of public attitudes, for its 2012 Living Together report, shows that more than 80% of British adults under 50 now support the proposal of same-sex marriage. (page 29)

- You can get a divorce if you have been married at least a year and your relationship has permanently broken down. (page 30)

- A couple who tie the knot on Valentine's Day in 2013 have a 39 per cent chance of divorcing during their lifetime. (page 31)

- 39% of parents didn't access any professional support when they separated from their partners, of whom 25% said it was because they couldn't find the right help or support or felt embarrassed. (page 34)

- It is estimated that one in three children in the UK will experience parental separation before the age of 16. (page 36)

Arranged marriage

A marriage that is arranged by the parents of the bride and groom. Arranged marriage is very different from forced marriage, because the bride and groom agree to the process.

Bigamy

Marrying more than one person. This is a criminal offence, punishable by law.

Child marriage

A cultural practice in which a child is forced to marry. Because of the importance placed on female virginity, the child is usually female and is forced to marry a man who is much older.

Civil partnership

The Civil Partnership Act 2004 created a scheme for the legal recognition of homosexual relationships. The Act applies to England, Scotland, Wales and Northern Ireland. Civil partnerships extend all the legal rights and privileges of marriage to homosexual couples.

Cohabitation

People in an intimate relationship who live together. In the eyes of the law, cohabiting couples do not have the same rights as married couples (for example, a couple who are cohabiting do not qualify to be each others' next of kin).

Common law marriage

Many people believe that a marriage-like relationship can be established simply by cohabiting for an extended period of time. In legal terms, this is not true. Cohabitation does not lead to the same rights as marriage.

Divorce

The legal separation of husband and wife.

Forced marriage

When a bride or groom is forced into marriage against their will. Physical violence and emotional abuse are often used in order to force the reluctant party to comply.

Marriage

When a man and a woman join together in a close and intimate union that is recognised by law, becoming husband and wife. In the UK, the legal age at which you can marry is 18-years-old, or 16- to 17-years-old if you have parental consent.

Marriage (Same Sex Couples) Bill 2012–13

Currently, same-sex marriage is not permitted under UK law. The Same Sex Couples Bill aims to introduce civil marriage for same-sex couples in England and Wales. Some argue that same-sex marriage will 'weaken the institution of marriage', while others are strongly in favour of the Bill. The Same Sex Couples Bill would also allow homosexual couples to wed in religious ceremonies, if the registered buildings/ premises agree.

Monogamy

Monogamous relationships involve just two partners.

Polygamy

Relationships that involve more than two people. For example, having more than one spouse.

Prenuptial agreement (pre-nup)

A contract entered into by the two people before they are married or enter into a civil union together. A prenuptial agreement functions as an insurance policy, detailing how assets would be divided in the case of a separation.

Assignments

1. In small groups, brainstorm to find out how much you know about marriage. Create a mind-map of your ideas on a large piece of paper, then feedback to the rest of your class.

2. Choose a religion and research its marriage traditions. Create a presentation that explains and demonstrates your chosen religion's marriage customs. Try using pictures, music or video to make your presentation exciting and engaging.

3. Read the articles *How marriage has changed over centuries* on page 4 and *Marriage and partnership: legislative landmarks* on page 5. Write an article for your local newspaper called *The evolution of marriage*, in which you summarise how marriage has changed over time.

4. Look at the graphs on page 7. Conduct a similar survey within your class or year-group to find out what they believe is the ideal age to get married. Create a graph that compares male and female responses then write a summary of your findings.

5. Divide into small groups and script a radio show in which the host is asking listeners 'What is the point of getting married? Why not just live together instead?' One member of your group should play the part of the radio host and the others should call-in to voice their opinions.

6. Read *Facts about forced marriage* on page 12. Now, imagine that you are in the following situation: your friend Yasmin has told you that her parents want to take her to visit their home country, so that she can learn more about her family's history and culture. Yasmin confides in you that she fears her parents intend for her to marry a man she has never met while they are away. Write a bullet point list of the steps you could take to help Yasmin. Include organisations that she could turn to for advice.

7. Create a campaign that will raise awareness of the issue of child marriage. Your campaign could take the form of television ads, banners that would appear on social networking sites such as Facebook, or even posters on the London Underground network. Produce a campaign plan and samples.

8. Write a blog post explaining the difference between civil partnership and same-sex marriage. In your post, you should also consider whether civil partnership should be offered to heterosexual couples as well as homosexual couples.

9. Read *Ten reasons why the Government is wrong to redefine marriage* on page 21. Choose one of these reasons and construct a short paragraph arguing against it.

10. Create a map of the world and colour code each country according to their laws surrounding same-sex marriage.

11. Create a questionnaire that will ask people about their opinions on same-sex marriage. You should ask respondents to indicate their age and sex, then analyse your results. Are young people more open minded than older people? Is there a difference between male and female opinions? Write a summary of your findings and briefly report back to your class.

12. Design an advice leaflet for married couples, or those in a civil partnership, wishing to get divorced. What steps do they need to take? Where can they seek further advice?

13. With a partner, imagine you are about to get married. Draft a pre-nuptial agreement, then think about whether you think they are a good idea or a bad idea.

14. In small groups, discuss the meaning of marriage. Make notes on your discussion and then write a dictionary definition of the word 'marriage'. Compare your definitions with those of other groups.

15. Design a website that will offer help and advice to children whose parents are getting divorced. Produce a plan for your website and some sample pages.

16. Write an advice guide for couples who are living together and do not intend to get married. What are the financial implications of this situation? What might couples need to be aware of if they separate?

17. Research marriage ceremonies in the Victorian era. What did a traditional ceremony involve? Do we still practise these traditions now? Write a summary of your findings.

Acknowledgements

The publisher is grateful for permission to reproduce the following material.

While every care has been taken to trace and acknowledge copyright, the publisher tenders its apology for any accidental infringement or where copyright has proved untraceable. The publisher would be pleased to come to a suitable arrangement in any such case with the rightful owner.

Chapter 1: Marriage & cohabitation

Getting married © Citizens Advice 2013, *How marriage has changed over centuries* © The Week Publications, Inc. 2013, *Marriage and partnership: legislative landmarks* © OnePlusOne 2013, *What do women want? To be married of course* © Telegraph Media Group Limited 2013, *The myth of common law marriage* © OnePlusOne 2009, *Distinctive features of marriage* © The Marriage Foundation 2013, *Is pro-marriage campaign on firm foundations?* © AOL (UK) Limited, *Facts about forced marriage* © Crown Copyright 2013, *Child marriage: a global problem* © Population Reference Bureau 2013.

Chapter 2: Same sex marriage?

What is civil partnership? © Cornwall Council 2013, *You're gay, you're in love, you want to be together forever ... get hitched!* © Stonewall 2013, *Marriage and family: civil partnerships* © The Christian Institute 2013, *Marriage (Same Sex Couples) Bill* © Crown Copyright 2013, *Same Sex Marriage Bill storms through House of Commons* © Stonewall 2013, *Ten reasons why the Government is wrong to redefine marriage* © Coalition for Marriage 2013, *Same sex marriage: mythbuster* © Crown Copyright 2013, *Marriage for all: it's time for civil partnerships to go* © Telegraph Media Group Limited 2013, *But why would anyone want to get married?* © independent.co.uk 2013, *Gay people divided over same-sex marriage* © ComRes 2013, *Religious Britons support gay marriage* © 2000 – 2013 YouGov plc.

Chapter 3: Divorce

Ending a marriage or civil partnership © Crown Copyright 2013, *Startling new research on UK divorce rate* © The Marriage Foundation 2013, *Teens and divorce: the kids are not all right* © independent.co.uk 2013, *Government launches divorce app* © Crown Copyright 2012, *DIY divorce comes with a health warning* © divorce.co.uk 2013, *Children affect by separation* © OnePlusOne 2012, *The benefits of being divorced* © Kimberly Seltzer 2013, *Trapped: the former couples who can't afford to move on* © Guardian News and Media Limited 2013.

Illustrations:

Pages 1 & 29: Don Hatcher; pages 16 & 34: Angelo Madrid; pages 14 & 32: Simon Kneebone.

Images:

Cover and pages iii & 25 © iStockphoto.com, p.3 © Michael Zacharzewski, p.10 © Eva Katalin, p.23 © Diana Lundin Photography, p. 36 © Ulrica Törning.

Additional acknowledgements:

Editorial on behalf of Independence Educational Publishers by Cara Acred.

With thanks to the Independence team: Mary Chapman, Sandra Dennis, Christina Hughes, Jackie Staines and Jan Sunderland.

Cara Acred

Cambridge

May 2013